THE WEIGHT OF EXISTENCE

The Weight of Existence

Poems on Mental Health

Joel Hawksley

J & Washington Network

CONTENTS

To Hope: The Anchor in the Storm

This book is dedicated to Hope. Not a fragile, fleeting wish, but a powerful current that carries us through life's roughest waters. It's the anchor that holds us steady when the storms rage, the compass that guides us when the path ahead is unclear.

For those of you who share my faith, you might say Hope is the very essence of God's love, a burning ember that warms the soul with the promise of better tomorrows. It's the unwavering belief that even in the darkest night, dawn will come.

But Hope is for everyone. It transcends religion, culture, background – it's a universal human language. It's the flicker of possibility that ignites a fire within us, urging us to take that next step, even when doubt whispers in our ear.

These poems are all whispers of Hope, testaments to its enduring power. They're written from the trenches of doubt and despair, but they all reach for that light at the end of the tunnel.

This book is for anyone who has ever felt lost or grappled with the shadows. It's a testament to the strength of the human spirit and a reminder that hope can always be found, even in the deepest valleys.

So, let these words be an encouragement. Let them be a beacon in the storm, a testament to the unwavering power of Hope. Because as long as we have Hope, we always have a tomorrow.

1

ECHOES IN THE HOLLOW

In the hollow chambers of the soul, where shadows twist and linger,

Among the fragments of time, broken and disjointed, there lies a wound,

A wound festering in the silent hours, echoing through the corridors

Of memory, a stark and relentless reminder of battles unseen.

We are the hollow men, in the valley of desolation,

Where each thought, each breath, is tinged with the residue of dread,

For in the night, the past whispers, haunting, spectral,

Drawing us into the vortex of our own despair.

Time present and time past,

Are both perhaps present in time future,

And the echoes of our torment stretch across the unseen abyss,

Where the wheel of suffering turns unceasingly, grinding hope to dust.

I have measured out my life with coffee spoons,

Yet each spoonful, each sip, is laced with the bitter taste of anguish,

The inescapable drone of remembered fear,

As the shadows stretch long and dark, consuming the light.

Between the idea and the reality, between the motion and the act,

Falls the Shadow, casting a pall over the fleeting moments of peace,

And in the stillness, in the dead of night,

We confront the ghosts of what was, what could have been.

This is the way the world ends,

Not with a bang but a whimper,

A whimper of the soul, exhausted by the relentless barrage of phantoms,

Seeking solace, yet finding only the hollow resonance of silence.

O dark night of the soul, in the interstices of our being,

Where the fragments of our lives lay scattered,

Let us find some fragment of peace, some whisper of redemption,

In the broken symphony of our existence.

2

SHADOWS OF THE MIND

In the shadowed depths where sorrow lies,
And phantoms tread with silent cries,
There dwells a torment, dark and grim,
A specter veiled, in shadows dim.

Within the mind, where nightmares creep,
And anguished souls no solace keep,
A tempest rages, fierce and wild,
A tortured heart, forever exiled.

The echoes of a distant war,
Resound within, forevermore,
A battlefield of blood and fear,
Where silent screams are all we hear.

Oh, cruel affliction, dark and deep,
You steal our peace, deny our sleep,
With memories that sear and burn,
And leave us broken, none return.

In haunted dreams, we walk alone,

Through corridors of dark unknown,
Where every step is fraught with dread,
And ghosts of past are always fed.

The mind, a prison wrought with pain,
Where sanity begins to wane,
And every moment's fleeting grace,
Is swallowed by the dark embrace.

If left to fester, unrestrained,
This madness grows, the soul is stained,
By whispers dark, and shadows vast,
A spirit crushed, by shadows cast.

Despair, a cloak that wraps us tight,
In endless corridors of night,
Where hope is but a distant gleam,
A fleeting wisp, a shattered dream.

O, mercy, grant us sweet release,
From endless night, a moment's peace,
Or else, in shadows we shall dwell,
In the torments of our private hell.

Thus, in the depths where sorrow lies,
And phantoms tread with silent cries,
We pray for light, for dawn's reprieve,
For hope, for life, for souls to cleave.

3

WHISPERS OF ETERNITY

In twilight hours, when shadows play,
And night consumes the fading day,
Thoughts of death, in whispers, speak,
Of realms beyond, both vast and bleak.

Where does the soul, in darkness, wend,
When life's frail thread comes to its end?
Does it rise on wings of light,
Or fall to depths of endless night?

In stillness deep, where echoes fade,
And silence casts its longest shade,
We ponder on the final breath,
The shroud of life, the face of death.

Do spirits roam in fields of green,
In lands unseen, where dreams convene?
Or drift in voids, with stars their guide,
In cosmic seas, where truths abide?

Is there a gate, a bridge, a door,

That leads us to the evermore?
Or do we blend with earth and sky,
In nature's cycle, never die?

These questions haunt the living mind,
With answers scarce, and truth confined,
Yet in our hearts, a hope persists,
That something more beyond exists.

For every end, a new beginning,
A tale untold, a life unending,
Where souls may find their destined place,
In realms of peace, in boundless space.

So, when the night grows dark and cold,
And whispers of the grave unfold,
Take heart, for in the mystery,
There lies the soul's eternity.

4

UNANSWERED TOMORROW

What of tomorrow, when I am gone,
When dawn breaks light, yet I move on?
Will birds still sing their morning song,
Or will the world feel something wrong?

Will shadows stretch and trees still sway,
In gentle dance to greet the day?
Will laughter ring, will hearts still play,
In the absence of my stay?

O unanswered tomorrow, so stark and vast,
What echoes linger from the past?
What whispers speak of moments cast,
In the light that fades so fast?

Will friends recall my smile, my voice,
In fleeting memories, a choice?
To hold me close, or let me drift,
Like autumn leaves, an endless rift.

Will flowers bloom with vibrant hue,
In gardens where my footsteps knew?
Or will they wilt, with petals strewn,
In silence, under skies of blue?

Unanswered tomorrow, tell me true,
What does the future hold, anew?
In spaces where my shadow fell,
Will life proceed, or pause and dwell?

Yet, as the world spins on its course,
With time, an ever-constant force,
I hope some joy, some love, remains,
In hearts I touched, in life's refrains.

For though I leave, the dawn still breaks,
And with each breath, new life awakes,
In every tear, in every cheer,
I linger, though I am not here.

Unanswered tomorrow, vast and wide,
In your embrace, my secrets hide,
But know, in every rising sun,
My essence lives, though I am done.

5

HOW WILL I?

Have you ever wondered, in silent night,
How you will face that final flight?
When breath grows still and eyes close tight,
What shape will death take, dark or light?

Will it be a whisper, soft and low,
A gentle fade, a quiet glow?
Or like a storm, with fierce decree,
Sweeping in with sudden spree?

Will it come in dreams, serene and kind,
A peaceful drift, a tranquil mind?
Or in shadows dark, with ruthless stride,
An unforeseen, swift turn of tide?

Will it be the slow decay of years,
Marked by aches and quiet tears?
Or the quick release of fate's cruel hand,
A swift departure, unplanned?

Perhaps it comes with nature's grace,

A final smile upon my face,
As twilight wraps in warm embrace,
And I dissolve without a trace.

Or will it be in battle fierce,
With courage strong and heart to pierce,
A life laid down with purpose clear,
For love, for truth, without a fear?

In moments lone, I've pondered this,
The end of life, the final kiss,
Yet knowing not what form it takes,
Each breath, each step, the mystery makes.

How will I die? I cannot see,
What fate or fortune holds for me,
But in the wondering, I find,
A deeper love for life, entwined.

So, as I walk this winding way,
Embracing night, welcoming day,
I'll live with passion, love, and sigh,
And let the future gently lie.

6

SHADOWS OF GUILT

In shadows cast by a screen's cold light,
A man sits alone, in the dead of night,
With guilt as his chain, and shame as his shroud,
In the silence, his thoughts are loud.

A heart heavy with burdens unseen,
A soul lost in a digital sheen,
Addiction's grip, a cruel embrace,
Leaves him hollow, an empty space.

He yearns for love, for touch, for grace,
Yet finds himself in a lonely place,
Where pixels dance and fantasies fade,
And real connections are betrayed.

Each moment spent in the depths of this vice,
Cuts deep like a blade, a personal slice,
Of a life that once was whole and pure,
Now tainted by desires obscure.

He seeks solace in fleeting frames,

In temporary highs, in burning flames,
But after the rush, the emptiness stays,
A constant reminder of wasted days.

The guilt, it gnaws, a relentless beast,
Feeding on moments, from greatest to least,
In mirrors, he sees a stranger's face,
In eyes that reflect a deep disgrace.

Unloved, he feels, in the quiet of night,
With no one to hold, to make it right,
The warmth of love seems far away,
In a world where shadows play.

Yet hope, a flicker, in the darkest of times,
Whispers of change, in soft, gentle rhymes,
To break the chains, to seek the light,
To find redemption, to end the fight.

For within the man, a heart still beats,
With strength to conquer, to face defeats,
To rise above, to heal, to mend,
To find true love, and a journey's end.

So, in the shadows, let courage bloom,
To break addiction's cruel, dark loom,
To seek the love that's always been,
Within himself, a new life to begin.

7

AFRAID OF EVERYTHING

In the shadows where the moonlight fades,
A tremor rises, fear invades,
Blood runs cold, as darkness spreads,
With whispered screams, and silent dreads.

Afraid of everything, the night, the day,
The lurking horrors that come our way,
The pain that sears, the wounds that bleed,
The suffering that follows every deed.

In the silence of a heart's deep ache,
Where nightmares slumber, poised to wake,
A breath is held, a pulse is quick,
As thoughts of terror crowd and stick.

The specter of the unknown prowls,
In the dead of night, as the wind howls,
With claws unseen, and eyes that glare,
It stalks the mind, it haunts the air.

The blood, it spills, a crimson stream,

In the waking world, in the twisted dream,
Where agony and fear entwine,
And every step is fraught with time.

Otherworldly dangers lie in wait,
Beyond the threshold of fate's gate,
Where shadows twist and voices wail,
In realms where sanity grows frail.

Afraid of everything, the touch of death,
The fleeting nature of each breath,
The silent void that lies ahead,
The creeping dread, the tears we shed.

Life's dangers coil, a serpent's hiss,
In every moment, in every kiss,
With eyes wide open, hearts confined,
We navigate the terror of the mind.

Yet in this fear, we find our way,
Through haunted night and dismal day,
For though the darkness presses near,
We stand and face the tide of fear.

Afraid of everything, we strive,
To find the strength, to stay alive,
For in the terror, in the strife,
We find the pulse, the beat of life.

8

THE WEIGHT OF THE WORLD

In shadowed realms where darkness breeds,
A youth with burdened heart proceeds,
With thoughts as heavy as the night,
And dreams that falter, taking flight.

Beneath the moon's pale, ghostly gleam,
In silent, sorrowed, haunted dream,
He treads the path of hidden fears,
His eyes reflecting unshed tears.

O, weight of world upon his back,
A specter's touch, a phantom's track,
Anxiety, its icy hand,
Grips tightly in this shadowed land.

Each breath a struggle, fraught with dread,
Each step a climb, though paths have fled,
Depression weaves its dark embrace,
An endless maze, an endless chase.

The laughter of his peers, a ghost,
An echo of what hurts the most,
For in their joy, his sorrow's clear,
A rift that grows from year to year.

O, heavy heart, so young, so frail,
With whispers dark, and spirits pale,
What solace can this world afford,
When shadows darken every word?

Yet in the gloom, a distant light,
A hope that pierces through the night,
For even in the darkest days,
A spark of life, a hopeful blaze.

In shadowed depths where darkness breeds,
A youth with burdened heart proceeds,
But in his soul, a strength is found,
To lift the weight that holds him bound.

9

ACHES AND PAINS UNSEEN

Aches and Pains Unseen, they dwell,
In chambers of the mind's deep well,
With unseen fingers, cold and keen,
They carve their marks, their shadows lean.

A twinge, a pang, the body sighs,
Yet no physician's searching eyes,
Can find the root of this despair,
For what they seek is hidden there.

In tangled thoughts and troubled dreams,
Where sorrow flows in silent streams,
Emotions cloak in fleshly guise,
A masked distress that underlies.

The Heart, it knows these burdens well,
It hears the toll of Sorrow's bell,
In every beat, a whispered woe,
A secret language, deep and low.

These Pains Unseen, they tell the tale,
Of Spirits worn and faces pale,
Of battles waged within the soul,
Where Mind and Body pay the toll.

No Bandage binds, no Pill can cure,
The subtle Grief we must endure,
For in the quiet, soft and still,
Resides the root of every ill.

Yet, through the Veil of Pain and Fear,
A Light of Hope can still appear,
To heal the wounds that lie beneath,
And bring the soul a sweet relief.

Thus, let us tend with gentle care,
The Aches Unseen that linger there,
For in the Mind's vast, shadowed space,
Resides the path to Healing's grace.

10

ERODED JOY

Once, on paths where sunlight played,
I found a joy in simple things,
In forests deep and meadows wide,
Where nature's song and laughter rings.

Yet now, those paths are worn and bare,
Their beauty lost to time's cruel hand,
The streams once clear, now muddy, gray,
And silence falls where song once spanned.

The fishing pond, where hours were spent,
With line and hook, a boy's delight,
Now lies untouched, a distant dream,
Its waters dark, devoid of light.

The fields where games and laughter bloomed,
In summer's golden, fleeting days,
Are shadows of their former selves,
With memories like autumn haze.

The books, the tunes, the tales untold,

That once inspired a fervent fire,
Now gather dust upon the shelves,
Their magic dulled, their sparks expired.

In winter's grasp, where frost and chill,
Have stripped the trees of all their green,
So too, has joy, eroded still,
Left barren scenes where life had been.

What cruel wind has swept this land,
What sorrow etched in heart and mind,
That joy, once bright as morning sun,
Is now but echoes left behind?

Yet in this loss, a quiet call,
A whisper through the lonely pines,
To seek anew, in hidden nooks,
The seeds of joy in life's confines.

For though the paths are rough and worn,
And shadows fall where light once lay,
The heart that seeks can still transform,
And find new dawns in each new day.

11

A FRAGILE HEARTBEAT

In the quiet of the night, a heartbeat frail,
Echoes through a body worn, a whispered tale,
Of anxiety's relentless grasp, its cold embrace,
A storm within, unseen, yet leaves its trace.

Each breath a struggle, each step a climb,
Through invisible chains, a dance with time,
The chest constricts, the pulse runs wild,
A grown soul trembles, feeling like a child.

O, fragile heartbeat, pounding in the dark,
Against the ribcage, a desperate mark,
Of unseen battles fought within,
Of silent cries and fears that spin.

The hands that tremble, the sweat that beads,
The racing thoughts, the unmet needs,
A mind in turmoil, a body's plight,
Both caught within this endless fight.

Anxiety, a thief of peace,

Leaves behind no sweet release,
But in the stillness, strength is found,
In every beat, in every sound.

For in the heart that feels so weak,
Lies a power, a voice to speak,
Of courage in the face of dread,
Of standing tall, though filled with lead.

O, fragile heartbeat, know your worth,
In the vast expanse of this great earth,
For though anxiety may take its toll,
It cannot dim the strength of soul.

So breathe, dear heart, through night and day,
Find the light amidst the gray,
For in each pulse, in every beat,
Lives the spirit, fierce and fleet.

With every tremor, every sigh,
Know that you have wings to fly,
Through the storm and past the night,
Into the dawn's forgiving light.

12

RESTLESS NIGHTS

In the velvet shroud of midnight's embrace,
Where shadows dance with whispered grace,
I lie awake, with mind afire,
In the realm where dreams expire.

The clock ticks on with mocking glee,
Each second echoes, tormenting me,
As sleep eludes with cruel intent,
Leaving me in restless torment.

A specter haunts my fevered brow,
With every sigh, I wonder how,
The night extends its cold embrace,
And I'm trapped in this endless chase.

The moon, a silent, watchful eye,
Betrays no solace as it drifts by,
Its pale light mocks my weary plight,
In the lonely hours of the night.

Oh, restless nights, relentless foe,

Your grip upon my soul does grow,
In tangled sheets, I twist and turn,
As the fires of insomnia burn.

No peace, no respite, no relief,
From the turmoil that steals my belief,
In sanity's grip, now slipping fast,
Into the abyss of sleepless cast.

Oh, to dream, to find release,
From this ceaseless mental lease,
But in the darkness, I remain,
In the throes of insomnia's reign.

13

DREAMS OF ESCAPE

I dream of sleep, a velvet shroud,
Where thoughts may rest, away from crowd,
In realms where time suspends its flight,
And shadows dance in silent night.

Excessive slumber, soft and deep,
A refuge found in dreamy keep,
Where troubles fade, and worries cease,
In the embrace of sweet release.

The world outside, a distant land,
Where chaos reigns, and voices stand,
In contrast to the quiet bliss,
Of dreams that drift, in gentle kiss.

To close my eyes, and drift away,
Where fantasies in colors play,
A fleeting escape, from reality's grasp,
In dreams, I find my peace at last.

No burdens weigh upon my brow,

No chains to bind, no questions now,
In sleep's sweet sanctuary, I find,
A solace deep, for heart and mind.

Yet waking comes, with harsh refrain,
Reality's grasp, it pulls again,
But in my dreams, a place to roam,
Where I find solace, and a home.

14

HOPELESS HORIZON

O vast expanse, where shadows loom,
In the boundless reach of night's deep gloom,
A soul adrift on a darkened sea,
Seeking a light that cannot be.

In this great wilderness of thought,
Where hope seems but a dream forgot,
The horizon fades to endless black,
And every step feels off the track.

The heart, it yearns for dawn's embrace,
For a glimpse of light, a saving grace,
Yet darkness holds its firm command,
In a world that seems so desolate, so grand.

O comrades, wanderers of this night,
Who tread the path without a sight,
I feel your weight, your heavy sigh,
As we seek the stars in a clouded sky.

The hopeless horizon, stretching wide,

In the depths of the soul, where shadows bide,
A mirror of the inner strife,
A portrait of a shattered life.

Yet within this dark, there lies a song,
A whisper faint, a call to strong,
To lift our eyes, to seek anew,
For in the struggle, courage grew.

For though the night is deep and vast,
And hopeless seems to bind us fast,
Within our hearts, a fire remains,
A spark that defies the dark's domains.

O, hopeless horizon, I challenge thee,
For within my soul, I am free,
To fight, to strive, to find the way,
And greet the dawn of a new day.

15

FADING APPETITE

In the quiet kitchen's muted light,
Where shadows blend with soft twilight,
I sit alone at table's edge,
And feel a hunger's faintest wedge.

The plate before me, laden well,
With sustenance from nature's swell,
Yet appetite, once full and bright,
Now fades within the evening's light.

Each morsel seems a distant chore,
A burden where delight's no more,
The joy of taste, a memory,
Lost in a fog of lethargy.

For depression, like a winter's chill,
Has stilled my heart, has dulled my will,
And in its grasp, I find no cheer,
No craving for the feast set here.

The bread I break is dry and stale,

The wine, it sours in its pale,
The fruits of labor, ripe and sweet,
Are bitter now, and incomplete.

How strange that sorrow can erase,
The simple pleasures of this place,
Where once I dined with eager heart,
Now I sit, a world apart.

Yet in the depths of this despair,
There lies a hope, a whispered prayer,
That spring will come, with warmth and light,
And bring again my lost delight.

For seasons turn, as they must do,
And with them, life is born anew,
So though today my appetite fades,
Tomorrow's dawn may lift these shades.

And I, once more, may find the taste,
Of life's rich banquet, not to waste,
With heart restored, and hunger bright,
In the fullness of the day's delight.

16

THE HEAVY SILENCE

In the stillness of the night, where shadows lie,
A heavy silence lingers, like a mournful sigh,
Unspoken pain, a burden deep,
A secret kept, a wound to keep.

The walls, they listen, but they do not speak,
They feel the weight, they hear the creak,
Of hearts that break in quiet tears,
Of whispered fears and hidden years.

A child who smiles, but her eyes reveal,
A world of hurt, a pain that's real,
In laughter bright, a shadow stays,
A silent cry in her gentle gaze.

The man who walks with shoulders bowed,
Carries a silence, like a shroud,
In every step, a story told,
Of battles fought, of courage bold.

The heavy silence shapes the day,

In subtle acts, in words we say,
It builds a wall, it draws a line,
Between the soul and what's benign.

Yet in this silence, strength resides,
A quiet power that never hides,
For though the pain is held within,
The spirit fights, it will not thin.

The unspoken pain, it molds, it scars,
But does not break, like fragile jars,
It teaches us to stand, to grow,
To find the light in shadows low.

So let us honor this silent strength,
This heavy silence, with all its length,
For in the stillness, truth is found,
In every heart, a beating sound.

We rise above the silent night,
We speak our pain, we find our light,
For though the silence may be deep,
It is not ours alone to keep.

17

FRACTURED FOCUS

In the dim-lit corridors of thought,
Where shadows twist and ideas rot,
I wander lost in fractured schemes,
Amidst the echoes of shattered dreams.

A mind once sharp, now clouded, gray,
With concentration led astray,
By specters of distractions foul,
That in the silence, softly prowl.

The quill lies idle in my hand,
Words drift like grains of shifting sand,
And every task, a mountain steep,
With valleys dark and caverns deep.

O, fractured focus, cruel fiend,
You steal the clarity I've gleaned,
Each moment splintered, torn apart,
By whispers that assail the heart.

The simplest chore becomes a plight,

A labyrinth of day and night,
Where thoughts do scatter, aimless, wild,
And patience flees, a frightened child.

In daily life, a ceaseless storm,
Where chaos reigns in varied form,
The mind, it wanders far and wide,
And leaves resolve cast aside.

Yet in this fractured, troubled state,
There lies a struggle, small but great,
To harness will, to find the thread,
To weave the thoughts that lie ahead.

For in the darkness, faint and rare,
A glimmered hope, a spark of care,
To mend the rift, to heal the mind,
And leave the shattered past behind.

O, fractured focus, yield to me,
Grant the peace of clarity,
That I might find my way anew,
With steady hand and vision true.

In the shadows where I roam,
I seek the light to guide me home,
To still the storm, to calm the sea,
And find the strength to simply be.

18

THE INVISIBLE ENEMY

In the caverns of the mind, where shadows creep,
An unseen foe in silence weeps,
It whispers dark, it prowls unseen,
In realms where fear and sorrow keen.

O, invisible enemy, lurking near,
You weave your web of doubt and fear,
In corridors where light is dim,
You plant your seeds, both thick and grim.

With spectral hands, you clutch the heart,
And tear the fragile soul apart,
Your presence felt in every sigh,
In whispered dread, in tearful eye.

How do I battle what I cannot see?
This phantom of my misery,
It twists my thoughts, it clouds my sight,
And drags me into endless night.

In moments quiet, it takes its hold,

In solitude, its tale is told,
Of terrors past and fears to come,
Of silence where the soul grows numb.

O, cruel specter, unseen foe,
How deep your talons in me go,
You steal the light, you veil the day,
And turn my mind to shadows gray.

Yet in this darkened, haunted maze,
I seek the light of brighter days,
To banish you, to break your chain,
And free my mind from endless pain.

For though you lurk in shadowed hall,
I hear the distant hopeful call,
Of strength within, of battles won,
Of dawn that breaks with morning sun.

Invisible enemy, hear my cry,
Though unseen, I'll not comply,
With every breath, I stand to fight,
And bring my soul into the light.

In caverns deep, where shadows lay,
I fight you off, I find my way,
For in the heart where courage lives,
No foe unseen forever thrives.

19

BENEATH THE SURFACE

beneath the calm (of)
        a smile's gentle curve
lies
    (oceans) of whispers
        (storms) of unheard cries

the (surface) serene
        like a mirror's gleam
while (beneath)
        the heart pounds
            with silent screams

in the quiet (of)
        an untroubled gaze
(fireworks) of sorrow
        blaze

the world sees (only)
        what it wants to see
a tranquil (face)
        a tranquil (sea)

but (beneath)
          the surface
lies
          the (truth)

a fragile (soul)
          a wounded (youth)

battles (fought)
          in shadows
          unknown
tears (shed)
          in silence
          alone

for (beneath) the calm
          and (behind) the grace
a storm (rages)
          in a hidden (place)

and in that (place)
          where (no) one sees
a heart (struggles)
          to find its (peace)

to the world, a (smile)
          a gentle (light)
but (beneath) the surface
          a quiet (fight)

20

STORMS WITHIN

There's a tempest brewing in my mind,
A storm unseen by those around,
A chaos that no peace can find,
Where anxious thoughts in circles bound.

The calm facade, a mask I wear,
To hide the turbulence inside,
For no one sees the dark despair,
The storm that never will subside.

The wind of worry howls and screams,
Through every corner of my soul,
It shakes the walls of silent dreams,
And leaves me feeling less than whole.

The lightning strikes of sudden fear,
Illuminate the darkest night,
They flash and vanish, sharp and clear,
Leaving echoes of their light.

And in this storm, I am alone,

A castaway in my own sea,
Tossed by waves of the unknown,
Adrift in my uncertainty.

Yet through the storm, I still must go,
To navigate the path unseen,
To find the strength I need to know,
And make my way through what has been.

For in the heart of every storm,
There lies a space of quiet, calm,
A moment where the soul can warm,
And heal its wounds with nature's balm.

So though the storm within me rages,
And peace feels like a distant shore,
I'll write my fears on empty pages,
And face the storm forevermore.

21

BREAKING THE CHAINS

In the depths of night, where shadows weave,
A soul cries out, "I must believe,"
In freedom from the chains that bind,
In light that heals a troubled mind.

The grip of pain, it holds me tight,
In darkness, steals away my light,
Yet in my heart, a fire burns,
A strength that grows, a hope that yearns.

I rise against the whispered lies,
That tell me I can't touch the skies,
I fight the weight that drags me down,
And wear my courage like a crown.

These chains of anguish, cold and stark,
Have left their mark, both deep and dark,
But in my spirit, fierce and strong,
I find the will to right the wrong.

With every step, I break a link,

In every tear, I dare to think,
That I can soar above this pain,
And dance beneath the healing rain.

For I am more than what you see,
A soul that's longing to be free,
To cast aside this heavy shroud,
And sing my truth, both clear and loud.

The path is rough, the journey long,
But I am filled with warrior's song,
With every breath, I claim my space,
And rise to meet the dawn's embrace.

Breaking the chains that held me back,
I find my way along the track,
To freedom's door, to open wide,
And greet the world with arms untied.

In every heartbeat, there's a beat,
Of liberation, pure and sweet,
For I am free, and I am whole,
A testament to a resilient soul.

22

TEARS UNCRIED

Tears, uncried, in silent flight,
Dwell in shadows of the night,
Veiled behind a steadfast guise,
Hidden deep from prying eyes.

In the heart, a weight does bear,
Of sorrows held, a silent prayer,
A grief that knows no outward show,
A storm within, where none may go.

Emotions bridled, held so tight,
Deny the soul its truest light,
The weeping willow, bent with strain,
Yet outwardly appears so plain.

The petals of the rose may fall,
Yet no one sees the tears at all,
For in the garden, blooms still grow,
Though roots beneath may twist in woe.

What cost, this silence, does it bring?

A muted song, a clipped-winged thing,
The echoes of a cry restrained,
In chambers of the heart remain.

But tears uncried, though softly kept,
In midnight's watch, they have not slept,
They shape the soul in quiet ways,
And color all the waking days.

For every tear that is unshed,
A deeper wound, a heavier tread,
The spirit bends, but does not break,
Yet bears the marks of its heartache.

So let the tears, like rivers, flow,
Release the flood, the undertow,
For in their course, the heart may find,
A softer rest, a peace of mind.

In the release of sorrow's tide,
The soul may heal, the heart may bide,
And in the morning's gentle grace,
Find solace in its own embrace.

For tears uncried are whispers frail,
Of unspoken tales, a secret trail,
Yet in their fall, they cleanse, renew,
The silent storms the heart once knew.

23

ACHING SOUL

O vast, immense, unyielding night,
Where stars above in silence gleam,
My soul, an ocean deep in plight,
Aching in an endless dream.

In every fiber of my being,
A sorrow lingers, shadowed, cold,
A weight upon my spirit, freeing,
Yet binding me in whispers old.

I wander fields of golden grain,
Yet feel the darkness in my core,
The beauty round me cannot gain,
A foothold on this weary shore.

Leaves of grass, they sway and bend,
In harmony with earth's own breath,
But in my heart, no peace does lend,
Only the ceaseless ache of death.

I sing the body electric, true,

Yet in my veins, a leaden flow,
A melancholy, deep and blue,
In every step, in every glow.

O comrades, kindred, passersby,
Do you see the shadow in my eyes?
Do you hear the silent, mournful cry,
In the echo of my softest sighs?

For I am he who walks the path,
With head held high and heart concealed,
Who feels the storm's relentless wrath,
Yet outward shows a visage healed.

In every dawn, a hope does rise,
In every dusk, a dream does fall,
But in my soul, the echo lies,
Of a pain that touches all.

O life, O death, O endless dance,
I seek the solace in your flow,
To find within your vast expanse,
The peace I crave, the truth to know.

Yet still I walk, with heavy stride,
Among the living, breathing throng,
And in my chest, this ache I hide,
In whispered verse, in silent song.

For though the pain is deep and wide,
An aching soul, a heart confined,
I find my strength in nature's tide,
And in the love of humankind.

24

VOICES OF DOUBT

In the obsidian depths of night,
Where shadows creep and fears take flight,
There lies a whisper, soft yet clear,
The voices of doubt I dread to hear.

Within my mind, a relentless choir,
Fanning the flames of a smoldering fire,
They speak of failure, loss, and shame,
And haunt my thoughts with cruel acclaim.

"Who are you," they hiss, "to dream so high,
When all your efforts merely die?
What worth have you in this grand scheme,
But a fleeting shadow, a broken dream?"

Their words, like daggers, pierce my soul,
They twist the knife, they take their toll,
Each echoing doubt, a crushing weight,
That binds me to a dismal fate.

I wander halls of memory,

Where every flaw, I clearly see,
Their voices rise in dark refrain,
Reminding me of past disdain.

Yet still I strive, in trembling fear,
To rise above, to persevere,
Though voices mock and shadows leer,
I seek a light, a path made clear.

For in the darkness, hope resides,
A beacon where true courage hides,
To silence doubt, to quell the storm,
To find within a strength reborn.

O voices of doubt, you shall not win,
For in my heart, resolve begins,
Though whispers haunt and shadows lie,
My spirit's flame will not yet die.

I cast you out, with weary breath,
And stand against your tales of death,
For though you seek to drag me down,
I wear defiance as my crown.

In the obsidian depths of night,
I forge my path, I claim my right,
To dream, to strive, to rise anew,
Beyond the doubt, beyond the blue.

So hear me now, O voices cruel,
In this dark game, I am no fool,
For though you whisper in the night,
My heart shall rise, my soul shall fight.

25

FLEETING HOPE

In the hollow hush of twilight's breath,
Where shadows stretch and time suspends,
There lies a flicker, faint yet bright,
A moment's hope, a brief amends.

The world, it seems, in that brief span,
To soften, lighten, shift its guise,
A fleeting glimpse of what could be,
A dream reflected in tired eyes.

Yet as the dawn retreats to dusk,
And silence wraps its shroud once more,
That fragile light begins to fade,
A memory of what's come before.

The whispered promises of peace,
The touch of grace upon the heart,
They wane like echoes in a void,
Like distant stars, they fall apart.

For hope, it seems, a transient guest,

In rooms where sorrow long has dwelled,
A visitor who stays a breath,
Then vanishes, its tale withheld.

The aching heart, it knows this well,
The ebb and flow of joy and pain,
The transient beauty of the rose,
That withers in the autumn rain.

Yet in this dance of light and dark,
A lesson lies, both hard and true,
That even in the darkest night,
A fleeting hope can see us through.

Though brief, its touch can warm the soul,
A spark within the coldest gloom,
A whisper of a brighter day,
A flower in the desolate room.

So let us cherish what we can,
These moments, fleeting though they are,
For in their light, however brief,
We find the strength to travel far.

In shadows deep, we hold this truth,
That hope, though fleeting, still can shine,
A beacon in the weary night,
A glimpse of something more divine.

26

THE MASK WE WEAR

O fair deceits, the masks we dare to don,
To veil the tempest roiling deep within,
We play our parts till night's pale moon is gone,
And hide our truths beneath a crafted grin.

Upon the stage of life, our roles are set,
With painted smiles and laughter's hollow sound,
Yet in our hearts, the anguished cries beget
A sorrow vast, where silence does abound.

The jester's cap, the monarch's golden crown,
The lover's gaze, the warrior's steely guise,
All but a semblance, lest we should drown
In tears unwept and grief that never dies.

O masks, ye cunning shields of fragile grace,
That guard the secrets of our mortal plight,
Beneath your charm, the shadows find their place,
And cloak the soul in ever-fading light.

What lies beneath the surface of our cheer?

What tempest lurks behind the calm façade?
The doubts, the fears, the ever-present tear,
The heart that bleeds in silence, deeply flawed.

Yet must we wear these masks, these veils of woe,
For who could bear to see the truth laid bare?
The depths of sorrow, none would wish to know,
The burdened soul, the cross it must declare.

But soft, the dawn reveals a tender hue,
A whisper of the truth we long to show,
For though the mask conceals, it cannot strew
The seeds of hope that through our spirits grow.

So let us find the courage, midst the strife,
To shed these masks, if but for moments brief,
To share our burdens, lightening the life,
And in our truth, discover sweet relief.

For in the naked visage of our pain,
There lies a beauty, raw and unconfined,
A testament to human frailty's gain,
The heart's endurance, and the strength we find.

Thus, shall we wear these masks, yet know the day,
When truth shall shine, and shadows fade away.

27

DESPERATE MEASURES

In the gloom of a room where the shadows loom,
There's a whisper, a murmur, a sigh of doom,
A mind in the grip of a desperate plight,
Turns to dark measures in the dead of night.

Oh, the tales it could tell, of the wretched and lost,
Of the paths that it chose, of the dreadful cost,
For when hope is but ashes, and light is but smoke,
A soul can be tempted by sinister folk.

There's a bottle, a needle, a pill in the drawer,
Each promising solace, but asking for more,
They whisper, "Come hither, forget all your pain,"
But the peace that they offer is hollow, inane.

In the murk and the mire, where the shadows conspire,
The heart seeks a refuge from thoughts that tire,
But the bottle is empty, the needle is cold,
And the promises fade as the story unfolds.

Oh, the deeds that are done in the quest for relief,

Leave a trail of despair, a forest of grief,
For the measures once taken in desperate haste,
Leave a bitter, enduring, and poisonous taste.

There's a darkness that grows when the spirit is weak,
When the silence is loud, and the future is bleak,
And the measures that seem to offer a way,
Are the steps into night, where the light fades away.

But within every heart, though it's battered and worn,
There's a spark of a dawn, of a day yet unborn,
If only to seek it, to grasp at the thread,
To find in the shadows the courage to tread.

For the measures of hope, though they're fragile and small,
Can rise from the depths where the desperate fall,
And the strength to resist the dark siren's song,
Can grow in the heart, where it truly belongs.

So heed not the whispers of measures unkind,
But seek in the night the dawn you may find,
For the battle within, though it rages and tears,
Can be won with the strength that a true heart dares.

28

THE ROAD TO NOWHERE

I've wandered long on this dusty road,
Where shadows lie and dreams erode,
A path that winds through fields of gray,
And leads my weary soul astray.

I've followed signs that promised gold,
But found the truth was harsh and cold,
The laughter's gone, the light's grown dim,
And hope has fled on fickle whim.

This road to nowhere, rough and wild,
Where once I strode with heart beguiled,
Now feels a cage of endless night,
A loop that binds with no respite.

The trees that once bore verdant leaves,
Now whisper tales of silent griefs,
The streams that sang in joyful glee,
Now murmur dirges, mournfully.

I've searched for answers in the sky,

In stars that twinkle, yet deny,
The secrets of this ceaseless trek,
This aimless, endless, joyless trek.

The cycle spins, a wheel of fate,
That traps the soul, that mocks the wait,
For peace, for joy, for sweet release,
For some small slice of inner peace.

Yet in the dusk, a thought does rise,
A glimmer in these darkened skies,
Perhaps this road, though bleak it seems,
Can lead me to forgotten dreams.

For though I'm trapped within this sphere,
A prisoner to my own dark fear,
There lies a strength within my breast,
To break these chains, to find my rest.

So onward still, through night and gloom,
I'll seek the dawn, I'll seek the bloom,
For somewhere on this road, I swear,
There lies a path to lead me there.

And though this road to nowhere winds,
I'll walk with hope that someday finds,
A place where shadows cease to reign,
And joy shall blossom once again.

29

WHISPERS OF PEACE

In the heart's deepest corners, where shadows reside,
There come whispers of peace, soft and untried,
Elusive moments, brief and rare,
A gentle breath in the silent air.

In the turmoil of the mind's endless flight,
Where chaos reigns both day and night,
A hush descends, a fleeting grace,
A tender touch, a soft embrace.

These whispers come like morning's dew,
A promise of calm, a world anew,
They linger just beyond our grasp,
Yet in their touch, our souls they clasp.

In the storm of thoughts, so wild and free,
They bring a moment's tranquility,
A breath, a sigh, a gentle pause,
A break in life's relentless laws.

They speak of hope, of love's pure light,

Of dreams reborn in the darkest night,
A melody that soothes the soul,
A piece of heart that makes us whole.

Though fleeting as the dawn's first ray,
They give us strength to face the day,
To hold within, through strife and storm,
The whispered peace that keeps us warm.

So listen close, when times are dire,
To whispers soft that lift us higher,
For in these moments, brief yet sweet,
We find the ground beneath our feet.

In every heart, a song does play,
A whisper of peace to light our way,
And though the calm may come and go,
Its touch remains, its grace we know.

For in the heart's deepest corners, where shadows reside,
There come whispers of peace, soft and untried,
And in those moments, brief yet true,
We find the strength to start anew.

30

THE SEARCH FOR LIGHT

In the labyrinthine corridors of the mind,
Where shadows stretch and secrets bind,
I wander through the maze of night,
On an endless quest for shards of light.

The dark is thick, it clings like tar,
Each step is heavy, each breath is scar,
A thousand whispers haunt my ear,
The echoing footsteps of my fear.

I seek the light, that fleeting beam,
That shimmers like a half-formed dream,
A spark to pierce this veil of black,
To guide me forth, to bring me back.

But the path is twisted, the way unclear,
The light retreats, it dances near,
Then fades to dark, a cruel jest,
Leaving me lost, an uninvited guest.

In this search, I've wandered far,

Past the ruins of who we are,
Through landscapes bleak, through storm and fire,
Driven on by a nameless desire.

For somewhere in this night's embrace,
Lies a glimmer, a saving grace,
A beacon bright, a silent call,
That promises an end to all.

Yet still I tread, though weary, worn,
Through fields of dusk, through realms of scorn,
For hope, though dim, still fuels my stride,
A stubborn flame I keep inside.

In this relentless quest for light,
I face the phantoms of the night,
I fight the demons that would bind,
To break the chains that twist the mind.

The search for light is never done,
It is a war that's never won,
But in the fight, a truth I find,
The light I seek, it lies inside.

For in each struggle, in each tear,
In every shadow faced in fear,
There grows a strength, a fierce delight,
A deeper, more enduring light.

So on this path, though dark and long,
I journey forth, I sing my song,
For in the heart of darkest night,
I find my way, I find my light.

31

SILENT BATTLEFIELDS

In silent battlefields of the mind,
Where no banners wave, no bugles call,
A war is waged, both fierce and blind,
Within the quiet, hidden thrall.

No soldiers' march, no cannons' roar,
Just the echo of a breathless fight,
Where courage falters, hope implores,
And shadows dance with morning's light.

Each day begins with the clash of steel,
Invisible to the untrained eye,
A conflict deep, intense, surreal,
Beneath the calm, a silent cry.

The foes are many, faceless, grim,
Doubt and fear, with icy hands,
They whisper secrets dark and dim,
In language only the heart understands.

These battlefields, so still, so stark,

Are littered with the scars of time,
Each wound a story, each shadow a mark,
Of wars unsung, of silent crime.

Yet in the midst of this quiet war,
There lies a strength, a spark of grace,
A resilience unknown before,
A warrior's heart in a fragile space.

For every battle fought and lost,
Is one step closer to the dawn,
Where victory is worth the cost,
And peace is more than a fleeting pawn.

So in these silent fields, we stand,
With unseen armor, shield, and sword,
We fight with mind, with heart, with hand,
Against the darkness, word by word.

No medals given, no parades,
Just the quiet satisfaction's gleam,
Of battles fought, of fears allayed,
In the silent battlefield's dream.

For though the wars are never done,
And peace is hard, a fleeting breath,
In every battle, there's a sun,
That rises from the night's cold death.

In silent battlefields of the mind,
Where no banners wave, no bugles call,
We find a strength, a will to bind,
And stand victorious, standing tall.

32

RISE FROM THE ASHES

Amidst the ruins of despair's grim hold,
Where shadows whisper secrets, dark and cold,
There lies a tale of courage, fiercely bold,
Of hearts that rise, though battered, through the old.

In valleys deep, where sorrow's echoes cry,
And every breath seems but a mournful sigh,
A spark ignites beneath the ashen sky,
A flame of hope that dares to not let die.

Through trials harsh and nights devoid of light,
Where every step seems fraught with endless plight,
There stirs a will, a spirit's guiding sight,
That leads the soul from dark into the bright.

From depths where once lay naught but silent screams,
Where dreams lay shattered, torn at hopeless seams,
Emerges strength, a river fed by streams,
Of resilience, a beacon's tender beams.

Each scar, a testament to battles won,

Each tear, a river that the heart has run,
Through storms that rage until the night is done,
There dawns a new, a fiercely rising sun.

For in the furnace of life's cruelest hour,
Where pain and loss seem all that dare to flower,
There blooms a strength, a deeply rooted power,
A phoenix rising from the ashen tower.

The journey, fraught with peril, grief, and strife,
Yet gives the soul a deeper, fuller life,
For every shadow faced with sharpened knife,
Carves out a path, through darkness, to the rife.

Of light that breaks through every battered wall,
Of hearts that learn to stand, though they may fall,
For in each fall, there's strength to heed the call,
To rise again, and walk the hero's hall.

So let the tale be told in whispered grace,
Of those who've journeyed through the darkest place,
To find the dawn, to see the morning's face,
To rise from ashes, to the light's embrace.

For in each heart, there lies a tale untold,
Of battles fought, of spirits fierce and bold,
And though the night may claim a bitter hold,
The rise from ashes is a tale of gold.

33

THE WEIGHT OF RESPONSIBILITY

In the grand and solemn hall of life,
Where duties intertwine and fate holds sway,
There rests upon the shoulders of our strife,
A burden great, the weight of every day.

The calls of work, the ceaseless, pressing chore,
Demand our time, our strength, our very core,
While family, with love and needs galore,
Requires the heart's deep, tender, fervent store.

Amidst these pulls, the self, oft cast aside,
Finds scarce a moment's peace, a place to hide,
Yet yearns for balance, seeks a calmer tide,
Where work, and home, and soul can coincide.

The office whispers in its urgent tone,
Its tasks, a never-ending, weary drone,
Yet in its call, a purpose lies unknown,
A duty borne, a seed of future sown.

At home, the laughter rings with pure delight,
Yet mingles with the tears in quiet night,
The joys and sorrows, blending, in their flight,
A symphony of life's own complex rite.

And there, within the heart's secluded space,
The self, a shadowed figure, runs its race,
To find amidst the chaos, a small grace,
A moment's rest, a fleeting, warm embrace.

The balance sought, a dance upon a wire,
A fragile step between the world's desire,
Yet in the striving, hearts are set afire,
With dreams of harmony that never tire.

For in this life, where every path demands,
We find the strength within our weary hands,
To juggle work, and love, and self's commands,
And build a life where each in balance stands.

So let us, in the face of life's great weight,
Find in our hearts the will to navigate,
The seas of duty, love, and self's own fate,
And carve a path where all may integrate.

For though the load is heavy, burdens great,
There lies within the power to create,
A life where balance finds its rightful state,
And peace and purpose walk through every gate.

34

THE LONG NIGHT

In the stillness of the witching hour,
Where shadows dance with spectral grace,
I find myself in sleep's lost tower,
Trapped within a restless space.

The clock ticks on, relentless, cold,
Each second drawn in tortured time,
A night that seems an age unfold,
A silent, ceaseless pantomime.

My thoughts, they race like lightning wild,
Through corridors of memory's hall,
A tempest fierce, a dream beguiled,
Where echoes of the past recall.

Insomnia, the tyrant king,
Commands the hours, rules the dark,
His silent reign, a bitter sting,
A throne within my weary heart.

I seek the balm of slumber's kiss,

The sweet release of dreams' embrace,
But every whisper, every hiss,
Keeps sleep's soft hand from my pale face.

The long night stretches on, it seems,
A journey through an endless void,
Where reason fades, and troubled dreams,
Are fragments of a mind deployed.

In this abyss, where silence roars,
The mind becomes a battlefield,
A place where every thought implores,
For solace that the night won't yield.

Yet in the depths of this dark plight,
A spark of hope begins to gleam,
For though I fight the endless night,
I hold within a waking dream.

A dawn will break, a light will rise,
To banish shadows from my sight,
For every night must meet sunrise,
And end the reign of sleepless night.

So through the long night, I will tread,
With weary heart and tired eyes,
For in the morn, where light is shed,
I'll find my peace beneath the skies.

And though the night is long and grim,
I know within, the dawn must come,
A hope that lights the darkest whim,
And brings the weary traveler home.

35

THE CRUMBLING MIND

Upon the isle where sun and sea embrace,
There lies a heart, a mind once clear and bright,
Now shadows gather in its sacred space,
And thoughts once sharp dissolve into the night.

Oh Muse, how swift the tides of time do change,
As sands erode beneath the ceaseless wave,
The mind, once vast, now feels so frail, so strange,
Its depths consumed by echoes of the grave.

The lyre's sweet song, now discordant and faint,
Once clear, now marred by whispers of despair,
The verses stutter, falter, and grow quaint,
As thoughts disperse like leaves in autumn air.

Where once the dawn brought visions pure and true,
Now mists obscure the edges of the day,
And memory, that faithful guide, eschews
The paths once trod, now lost in disarray.

Oh Aphrodite, grant me strength to bear

This slow descent into the shadow's hold,
For in this crumbling mind, I find my care,
A heart that strains against the growing cold.

The threads of thought unravel, lose their form,
As once bright patterns fade to muted gray,
The tempest in my mind, a brewing storm,
Sweeps clarity and focus far away.

Yet in the dusk, a fragile light remains,
A hope that glimmers through the thickening gloom,
For though the mind may crumble, break its chains,
The heart can bloom, e'en in its silent tomb.

So let the world behold my spirit's fight,
Against the fading of the inner flame,
For though the mind may yield to endless night,
The soul's resolve shall steadfastly proclaim.

In my voice, this lament softly sings,
Of minds that crumble, yet find strength in heart,
For even as the mind's bright light takes wings,
The soul endures, unbroken, set apart.

36

THE MASK OF NORMALCY

In the halls where shadows tread,
Where silent fears and whispers spread,
There lies a mask, of calm, composed,
A façade that hides what's undisclosed.

The eyes that sparkle, lips that smile,
A charade played with practiced guile,
Yet beneath the surface, storms do rage,
An unseen war within the cage.

The world beholds a tranquil face,
Unknowing of the inner chase,
Where thoughts like tempest wild do roam,
In a heart that feels so far from home.

This mask of normalcy, well-worn,
Conceals a soul both bruised and torn,
A careful craft of seamless guise,
That hides the depth of countless lies.

Each day, the mask is donned anew,

A shield against the world's cruel view,
Protecting from the prying gaze,
The fragile heart in darkened haze.

But oh, the weight, the heavy toll,
Of bearing burdens, hiding soul,
The strain of keeping shadows veiled,
While silently the spirit ails.

Behind the mask, the tears do fall,
In quiet nights, behind the wall,
Where no one sees the silent cries,
Or hears the pain in muffled sighs.

Yet in the dark, a voice does call,
A whisper soft, a gentle thrall,
To cast aside the mask once worn,
And face the world, though scarred and torn.

For in the truth, a freedom lies,
A strength unveiled, a clear sunrise,
To let the mask of normalcy fall,
And stand revealed, unguarded, tall.

In shadows deep, the mask was made,
A fortress built, a sad parade,
But in the light, the soul finds peace,
As masks are dropped and fears release.

So let the world see what's concealed,
The scars, the wounds, the heart revealed,
For in the truth, both raw and bright,
The soul can find its purest light.

37

SHATTERED DREAMS

In the gilded halls where dreams were spun,
Where aspirations gleamed like morning sun,
There lies a silent, somber place,
Where shattered dreams leave but a trace.

Once, with passion, hearts did soar,
Through skies of hope and visions' lore,
Yet now those dreams lie cold, unmet,
In shadows deep, where sorrows fret.

Depression, with its heavy hand,
Has cast a pall upon this land,
Turning vibrant goals to dust,
As ambitions fade and minds combust.

The brilliance of those dreams, once bright,
Now shrouded in the darkest night,
For every hope that dared to gleam,
Has fallen victim to this scheme.

No more the fervent, eager chase,

No more the striving, swift embrace,
For dreams lie broken, scattered wide,
With nothing left but hollow pride.

Yet even in this bleak domain,
Where loss and heartache stake their claim,
A flicker, faint, begins to rise,
A whisper of those bygone skies.

For dreams, though shattered, still remain,
In fragments small, amidst the pain,
And from these pieces, new dreams form,
In hearts that weather every storm.

Though goals may shift, and paths may veer,
The spirit's fire remains sincere,
And in the ruins of the past,
New aspirations bloom at last.

For life's true worth is not in dreams,
But in the heart that ever gleams,
With hope that, even through despair,
Finds strength to rise and still to care.

So let the broken dreams lie still,
And from their remnants, find the will,
To dream anew, to strive once more,
And build a future to adore.

In every shattered, lost ideal,
There lies a chance to start and heal,
To forge new paths, with courage rare,
And find the beauty hidden there.

38

ENDLESS WORRY

In shadowed realms where fears abide,
Where restless thoughts like tempests chide,
I wander through the night and day,
With endless worry as my guide.

The future looms, a spectral form,
A ceaseless, silent, swirling storm,
Each moment fraught with what might be,
A darkened sea where doubts are born.

What fate awaits in unseen hours?
What trials lie in hidden bowers?
These questions plague the weary mind,
A burden borne through life's brief flowers.

Each choice, each step, a weighty cast,
With every breath, the die is cast,
Yet in the grip of constant dread,
The present slips away too fast.

The mind, ensnared in anxious snare,

Seeks solace but finds naught but air,
For every path is shadowed, dim,
And peace, a ghost beyond compare.

Yet in this turmoil, soft and deep,
Where countless fears like serpents creep,
There lies a strength within the soul,
A flame that through the darkness peeps.

To face the future's shadowed veil,
With courage fierce and spirit hale,
To find within the strength to fight,
Against the worry's constant gale.

For though the future's shrouded still,
With unknown peaks and valleys fill,
The heart can find a steadfast course,
To navigate with iron will.

And in the quiet, calm and true,
Where moments of pure grace break through,
The endless worry fades to naught,
Replaced by hope in skies of blue.

So let the future come what may,
With all its shadows, bright or grey,
For in the heart that stands its ground,
The strength to weather all is found.

In endless worry's dark embrace,
The soul can find its saving grace,
To live each day with purpose clear,
And face the future without fear.

39

THE VOID WITHIN

Oft have I walked in shadowed vales of night,
Where silent winds of sorrow softly sigh,
And felt within a hollow, deep, and slight,
A void where once the heart did beat and fly.

This chasm vast, this empty, boundless space,
Where joy and sorrow both have fled away,
Leaves but a numbness on my weary face,
And dreams that fade like twilight's gentle ray.

No longer does the lark's sweet song delight,
Nor does the rose's bloom my senses stir,
For in this void, all beauty takes its flight,
And leaves me lost in shades of dulled amber.

The world, it moves with vibrant, ceaseless pace,
While I, a specter, drift through muted haze,
In search of warmth, of light, of love's embrace,
But finding naught in this unending maze.

Yet in this void, this hollow, silent sphere,

There lies a whisper, faint as morning's dew,
A promise that, though now I wander here,
The dawn may break, and bring the world anew.

For even in the depths of darkest night,
Where emptiness and numbness hold their sway,
The soul can find a spark, a glimmered light,
To guide it toward a brighter, kinder day.

So though the void within may chill and bind,
And numb the heart to all life's fleeting charms,
I seek the day when warmth again I'll find,
And rest my weary soul in gentle arms.

Till then, I walk through shadows long and deep,
With hope as fragile as a whispered prayer,
That someday soon, from this void's grasp, I'll leap,
And find my heart awakened, light, and fair.

40

ACHING HEART

In the quiet realms where shadows dwell,
Where the soul's deep murmurs softly swell,
An aching heart, with sorrow's stain,
Bears the weight of unrelenting pain.

This sadness, like an ancient tree,
Its roots entwined in memory,
Spreads through the veins with silent grace,
And leaves its mark on every place.

The mind, a vast and weary field,
To sorrow's scythe does slowly yield,
Each thought a burden, each breath a strain,
As sadness courses through each vein.

The body's frame, once strong and bright,
Now bends beneath this heavy plight,
The shoulders droop, the head bows low,
As tears, unbidden, freely flow.

Yet in this melancholy's hold,

There lies a strength, a quiet gold,
For in the depths of sorrow's sea,
The heart can find its liberty.

The aching heart, though bruised and torn,
Can rise anew with each new morn,
For sadness, though it takes its toll,
Cannot consume the resilient soul.

In nature's arms, a healing balm,
A whispered breeze, a gentle calm,
The heart can find a moment's peace,
And feel its burdens slowly cease.

For life, though fraught with pain and loss,
With trials that our paths may cross,
Is also filled with light and grace,
With beauty in each time and place.

So let the heart, though aching sore,
Find solace in the world's great lore,
And know that even in its pain,
It bears the strength to love again.

In every tear, a lesson learned,
In every sorrow, wisdom earned,
The aching heart, with time, will mend,
And find its joy in the journey's end.

41

THE SILENT CRY

In the stillness of the twilight's veil,
Where whispers of the night prevail,
There lies a cry, so soft, so faint,
A silent heart's unvoiced complaint.

Beneath the surface, calm and fair,
A storm of sorrows hidden there,
Emotions deep, suppressed, confined,
A restless sea within the mind.

The face, a mask of tranquil grace,
Conceals the turmoil's vast embrace,
While in the soul, a silent cry,
Yearns for release, for wings to fly.

The words unspoken, trapped in fear,
The eyes that hide each unshed tear,
The struggle of the heart and mind,
To find the voice that's left behind.

Oh, how the silent cry does ache,

In chambers where the echoes wake,
A longing for the world to see,
The pain that dwells in secrecy.

Yet in the shadows, strength is found,
A quiet force, profound, unbound,
For in the depths of silent night,
The heart prepares to face the light.

With every sigh, a whispered plea,
A hope that someday, courageously,
The silent cry will find its sound,
And voice its pain with truth unbound.

In nature's arms, a gentle balm,
The wind's soft kiss, the river's calm,
The silent cry finds space to breathe,
And slowly, surely, pain does leave.

For every heart that holds its pain,
A time will come, a gentle rain,
To wash away the fears and woes,
And let the soul in freedom flow.

So let the silent cry be heard,
In whispered breath, in spoken word,
And know that in the telling, free,
The heart will find its melody.

In the embrace of night and day,
The silent cry will find its way,
To rise above, to voice, to sing,
The song of pain's awakening.

42

LOST IN ROUTINE

In life's unending cycle, dark and deep,
Where days blend into nights without reprieve,
I find myself in paths that ceaseless keep,
A soul enshrouded, yearning to believe.

This endless round, where tasks repeat and bind,
A labyrinth of duties, pale and worn,
Leaves but a hollow echo in the mind,
A heart that's weary, tattered, and forlorn.

In mornings gray, where dawn brings naught but toil,
The sun's ascent seems but a distant light,
For in the mundane steps that ground and coil,
The spirit sinks into eternal night.

The hours, like shades of Purgatory's realm,
Move silently in measured, joyless tread,
A ship without a captain at the helm,
Adrift in seas where passions all have fled.

No voice of Virgil guides through this despair,

No Beatrice with light to pierce the gloom,
Just shadows cast by burdens we must bear,
In corridors of endless, silent doom.

The soul, entangled in this ceaseless grind,
Seeks respite in the fleeting dreams of sleep,
Yet wakes to find the chains that daily bind,
Still clamped upon the heart in hold so deep.

Yet in this void, a flicker faint and frail,
A spark that whispers of a brighter fate,
For even in routine's unyielding jail,
The heart can find the strength to liberate.

To break the chains of monotony's might,
To seek the stars beyond the dreary plain,
And in the quest for meaning, pure and bright,
Discover joy amidst the silent pain.

So let us rise, though weary be our frame,
And seek the paths where freedom's light does gleam,
For in the journey's end, we'll find the flame,
That wakes us from this numbing, endless dream.

Through my lens, the mundane finds a voice,
A call to break the chains, to seek, rejoice,
In life's divine and wondrous, boundless choice,
To turn routine into a path of choice.

43

ECHOES OF TRAUMA

Whan that Aprille with his shoures soote
Hath pierced to the roote our hearts' deep core,
The trauma's echo stirs, a silent note,
In minds where past and present intertwine, implore.

Whan Zephirus eek with his sweete breeth
Exhales the woes from times long passed away,
Yet still, within the soul, there lingers death,
Of joys, of peace, of life's once bright array.

In days of yore, the hurtful strokes were cast,
In bygone times, the wounds were deep and raw,
And though the years in haste have journeyed past,
The echoes of that pain still strike with awe.

The tales of sorrow in the mind replete,
Like Canterbury's pilgrims' varied lore,
Each step we take upon life's hasty street,
Reminds us of the scars we yet adore.

For in the dark recesses of our thought,

Where memories like phantoms do abide,
The echoes of old traumas ne'er forgot,
Resound with force, though we do often hide.

Yea, every laughter hides a tear unwept,
And every smile conceals a sigh unspoken,
For in the heart, where once sweet solace slept,
Now echoes of old traumas lie, unbroken.

Yet in this my world, both rich and wide,
Where tales of love and woe do intertwine,
We find in sharing, comfort to abide,
And solace in the fellowship divine.

For though the echoes of past pain do last,
And haunt the mind with shadows long and drear,
The strength to rise, to leave behind the past,
Lies in the bonds of kinship, strong and clear.

So let us journey forth with heart anew,
With courage drawn from fellowship so bright,
And though the echoes haunt, we shall construe,
A path through darkness, guided by the light.

In my words, we find a balm to heal,
A tale of hope amidst the echoes' cry,
For in our hearts, where deepest sorrows steal,
The strength to overcome does never die.

44

UNSEEN BATTLE

The world, a bustling tapestry of light,
Moves on, with all its brilliance, unaware,
While deep within, a battle's silent blight
Unfolds in shadows none can see or share.

The sunlit morning, bright with nature's call,
Casts golden beams upon the restless sea,
Yet in the heart, a darkness shadows all,
A hidden war that rages silently.

The face, a mask of calm and practiced grace,
Conceals the turmoil churning just below,
In public's gaze, no trace, no sign, no trace,
Of inner storms that silently bestow.

Each step, a fight against the heavy weight,
Each breath, a struggle none can comprehend,
The smile, a shield to guard the heart's own gate,
From questions that no answer could amend.

Beneath the surface, currents fierce and wild,

Sweep through the soul with whispers of despair,
While outwardly, the calmness is beguiled,
By unseen battles fought without a prayer.

The hands that tremble, hidden in the dark,
The eyes that glisten with unspoken tears,
The mind, a battlefield where thoughts embark,
On journeys wrought with shadows, doubts, and fears.

Yet in this unseen fight, a strength is found,
A quiet courage in the face of pain,
For though the world may never hear a sound,
The heart endures, and finds its peace again.

In solitude, the battle rages on,
A silent war that none may ever see,
Yet through the night, and till the break of dawn,
The soul persists, and claims its victory.

For in the unseen depths of private strife,
There lies a resilience, pure and true,
A testament to the enduring life,
That battles on, unseen by all but you.

45

FRACTURED FOCUS

In the rhythm of the city, fast and bright,
Where dreams are made beneath the neon light,
There lies a struggle, silent, deep, unseen,
A fractured focus in the urban scene.

My mind, it wanders like a vagrant's path,
Through alleys of distraction, fields of wrath,
The thoughts that once were clear now drift away,
Like autumn leaves on a forgotten day.

The work before me, tasks that never end,
Become a mountain I can't comprehend,
For every moment lost to fleeting thought,
Is a battle in this war that I have fought.

The jazz of Harlem, vibrant in the night,
A song of hope, of struggle, and of flight,
Yet here I sit, in shadows of my mind,
Unable to bring clarity, confined.

Each word I write, each sentence, every line,

Eludes my grasp, dissolving in the time,
For focus fractured leads to endless toil,
A fruitless labor in unyielding soil.

Oh, how I long for peace, a steady hand,
To guide me through this intellectual land,
But like the blues, my mind's refrain is slow,
A melancholy tune that ebbs and flows.

The city hums, a symphony of sound,
While I, in silent chaos, am bound,
To seek the threads of thought that slip away,
In the dawning of another restless day.

Yet in this struggle, there's a voice that calls,
A whisper in the night that softly falls,
"Keep pushing on," it says, "through all the strife,
For in your fractured focus, there's still life."

The dreams deferred, the hopes that never die,
Will find their way beneath the same bright sky,
And though the path is hard, and vision blurred,
The soul's resilience will not be deterred.

For in the heart of Harlem, strength abides,
A spirit that through all distraction rides,
And finds its way to clarity, to peace,
In the quiet moments, when the noise does cease.

So let the city sing its vibrant tune,
And I will find my focus, soon, so soon,
For in the struggle, there's a hidden grace,
A fractured focus finds its rightful place.

46

THE WEIGHT OF EXPECTATIONS

In this vast stage where all must play their part,
Beneath the gaze of countless watchful eyes,
A burden rests upon the beating heart,
A heavy weight that none may yet despise.

To meet the world's demands with steadfast grace,
To wear the mask of virtue, strength, and cheer,
While deep within, a turmoil finds its place,
A silent struggle veiled by outward veneer.

Society's call, a drumbeat loud and clear,
Commands a dance to which we must align,
Yet in the shadows, doubt and creeping fear,
Weigh down the spirit, tether the divine.

Expectations, like chains of polished gold,
Gleam bright but bind the soul with heavy hand,
They shape our steps, our stories yet untold,
And leave us yearning for a freer land.

The roles we play, the faces that we show,
Are but reflections of a greater whole,
Yet in the quiet hours, we come to know,
The toll it takes upon the seeking soul.

To please, to serve, to rise above the fray,
To be the paragon that others see,
Is to forego the self, to lose the way,
And dim the light of true identity.

Oh, what a weight to bear, what heavy cloak,
Of expectations draped upon the mind,
A yoke that chafes with every word bespoke,
And leaves the heart in restless search confined.

Yet in this strife, a truth begins to dawn,
That to be free, one must the chains unbind,
To cast aside the roles that we have drawn,
And seek the path that's true to heart and mind.

For in the self, unburdened and sincere,
Lies strength unyielding, courage to defy,
The weight of expectations, harsh and drear,
And soar beyond the limits of the sky.

So let the world its judgments harshly cast,
Let voices rise with their unending call,
The self, unbound, will find its way at last,
And stand, in truth, beyond the weight of all.

47

THE SILENT SCREAM

the silent scream of
        hearts unspoken
                whispers (aching) in
                        the night (alone)

where shadows dance
        with misunderstood
                echoes (lost in) twilight's
                bone

each breath a question
        (why) each sigh a
                plea (hear me)
                        but the world (turns

its back) unmoved
        the silent scream
                unheard (as stars)
                collide in

(darkness) dreams unravel

                    like ribbons
                        (caught in) winds
                            of time

the struggle to be
            seen (to touch)
                a soul with words (that
                    matter)

in a universe
            (so vast) where voices
                fade (into)
                    the scatter

of endless space
            yet still
                we scream
                    (in silent

hope) that someone
            (somewhere)
                feels the
                    beat

of our unheard
            hearts (the silent scream)
                a whisper (turns to)
                    light

in dreams where
            shadows (fade)
                to bright
                    and silence finds

its voice.

48

ECHOES OF LONELINESS

loneliness is a leaf
        falling
loneliness is a heart
    calling

  echoes of footsteps
echo
            lonely
    echoes

49

FACES IN THE CROWD

Amidst the throng where shadows blend,
And countless faces pass me by,
I wander lost, no hand to lend,
A solitary soul, a cry.

Their laughter rings, a hollow sound,
A distant echo in my mind,
For in this sea, where all are bound,
I am alone, no solace find.

The crowded streets, they weave a tale,
Of lives entwined, of hearts that beat,
Yet in this dance, I feel so frail,
A ghost that walks on unseen feet.

The eyes that glance, but do not see,
The whispered words, the silent screams,
They paint a world where none are free,
From loneliness that haunts our dreams.

I reach, I grasp, but touch is cold,

The warmth of human heart denied,
For though I'm here, the truth unfolds,
A world where none stand by my side.

In every face, a mask is worn,
In every smile, a secret hides,
The crowd moves on, and I'm forlorn,
A drifting soul on empty tides.

Yet in this vast, unyielding night,
A hope, a spark, begins to glow,
For even in the darkest plight,
A soul may find the strength to grow.

For faces in the crowd may blur,
But in the heart, a light can burn,
A beacon bright, a whispered stir,
A call for love, for hope's return.

So though I walk this path alone,
With shadows deep and silence loud,
I hold within a truth unknown,
There's life beyond the faceless crowd.

In solitude, I find my way,
Through darkened streets and empty halls,
For in my heart, the dawn of day,
Will break the night, the darkness falls.

For though the crowd may never see,
The soul that stands amidst their throng,
I find my strength, my liberty,
In knowing I am always strong.

So faces in the crowd, beware,
For I am not the ghost you see,
Within my heart, a fire rare,
A spirit strong, and ever free.

50

EMPTINESS

<pre>
a
hollow
     drum
          beats
               no
                    sound
</pre>

51

SHADOWS IN THE MIND

O, the shadows in the mind, where sadness lays its claim,

In the vast expanse of the self, a persistent, quiet flame,

From the bustling city streets to the silent country plains,

I hear the whispers of despair, in hearts bound by unseen chains.

O comrades, friends, and strangers, in this shared human plight,

We walk with burdens heavy, in the day and through the night,

In the boundless realm of thoughts, where hope seems but a dream,

I see the eyes of weariness, lost in a silent scream.

The world, so full of splendor, yet shadows still remain,

In the corners of our spirits, in the echo of our pain,

We seek the sunlit meadows, but the clouds obscure our view,

And the path of joy and light is hidden from our cue.

Yet in the depth of sadness, in the hopeless and the bleak,

There lies a thread of connection, for the weary and the weak,

O, the soul's profound endurance, in the darkest of the hours,

Through the shadowed veil of sorrow, still, the heart's wild flowers.

For in the song of sorrow, there's a cadence of the soul,

A rhythm born of heartache, yet striving to be whole,

In the whispers of the twilight, in the mourning of the dawn,

There's a spark within the darkness, and the spirit carries on.

O brothers, sisters, travelers, through this field of endless night,

Let us find our strength together, in the struggle, in the fight,

For in the collective heartbeat, in the joining of our hands,

We can turn the tide of shadows, and reclaim the hopeful lands.

So though the mind be shadowed, and the heart be sorely tried,

In the boundless human spirit, let our strength and hope abide,

For in the face of darkness, in the echo of the groan,

We find our deepest courage, and we know we're not alone.

52

FOG

<pre>
thought's
        slow
            dance
                 through
                      pea
                         soup
                            air
</pre>

53

THE INVISIBLE CAGE

Within my mind, an unseen cage,
A prison made of thought,
No bars of iron, nor locks to gauge,
Yet bound, ensnared, and caught.

In rooms of silent reverie,
I pace with footsteps light,
The echoes of my misery,
Resound in endless night.

A world outside, so vast and free,
While here, my spirit dwells,
Confined by unseen boundary,
In shadowed, silent cells.

The fields of green, the skies of blue,
Lie just beyond my reach,
For in my mind, a captive view,
To darkened corners leach.

No door to open, no key to turn,

No window to the day,
In this invisible cage, I yearn,
For light to guide my way.

The heart, it beats with muffled tone,
A rhythm dulled by fear,
In solitude, I stand alone,
With shadows ever near.

Yet in this cage of phantom steel,
A strength begins to grow,
A quiet hope, a will to feel,
The freedom I forego.

For though the bars are made of thought,
And locks of doubt and pain,
The spirit's wings are never caught,
By sorrow's cold domain.

In whispered breath, in silent plea,
I find a way to rise,
To break the chains that bind in me,
And reach for open skies.

The mind, a maze of shadowed walls,
Can also be the key,
To find the space where freedom calls,
And soul is truly free.

So in this cage, invisible,
I seek the light within,
To turn the lock, to pass the knell,
And let new life begin.

For in the heart's most secret place,
The strength to break is found,
The mind, unbound, can soar in grace,
Where once it was confined.

54

LETHARGY

    feet
of
   lead
      stairs
    a
daunting

   mountain

55

UNRELENTING DOUBT

In shadows deep where doubts reside,
A specter haunts my weary mind,
Unseen, yet felt with every stride,
A ghost that whispers, unkind.

Beneath the moon's pale, gentle light,
Where dreams take flight on wings of gold,
There creeps a fear, a dread of night,
A tale of worth, too oft retold.

Each step I take, each breath I draw,
Is fraught with whispers cold and grim,
"Unworthy, weak," the doubts do gnaw,
And fill my soul to every brim.

The stars above, in endless spread,
Seem distant, cold, and far away,
While in my heart, a ceaseless dread,
Turns night to dark and bright to gray.

Oft do I ponder, lost in thought,

The worth of deeds, the strength of will,
Yet find my courage come to naught,
In face of doubt's unyielding chill.

The pen, it trembles in my hand,
The words, they falter, weak and frail,
As if the muse could understand,
The weight of fears that yet prevail.

In every mirror, doubt reflects,
A visage pale, with eyes unsure,
A mind that constantly dissects,
Each flaw, each fault, too raw, too pure.

Yet in the depths of doubt's domain,
A flicker, faint, of hope does gleam,
A whisper soft amidst the pain,
A hint, a breath, a distant dream.

For though the doubts do ever press,
And shadows darken every thought,
The heart, in quiet, does confess,
A strength within, so dearly sought.

Through doubt, the soul does find its way,
Through fear, the heart its courage learns,
And in the night, where shadows play,
The spark of hope within still burns.

So let the doubts encircle round,
And fear its heavy mantle cast,
For in this struggle, strength is found,
And self-belief will reign at last.

In my words, this truth I find,
A solace deep, a quiet peace,
For though the doubt may bind the mind,
The heart's resolve will never cease.

56

DREAD

<pre>
a
                    cold
        coil
                    tightens
around
            the
                    heart
</pre>

57

THE SEARCH FOR PURPOSE

In midnight's depths, where shadows weave,
A tale of sorrow's dark reprieve,
I wander through the silent gloom,
A soul enwrapped in endless doom.

The raven's call, a haunting cry,
Echoes through the starlit sky,
While deep within, a question burns,
For purpose lost, my spirit yearns.

In halls where whispers softly tread,
The ghosts of dreams, long cold and dead,
Do murmur secrets faint and low,
Of paths I've lost, and truths I know.

Through corridors of endless night,
I seek a flame, a beacon bright,
To guide me from this shadowed land,
To places where the living stand.

Yet every step, a mournful sigh,
Each turn, a deeper, darker lie,
For in this quest for meaning's grace,
I find but mirrors, face to face.

Oh, cruel fate, that leaves me blind,
To wander in this maze of mind,
Where every corner hides despair,
And purpose seems a fleeting prayer.

The moon, a silent, watchful eye,
Doth see my heart's unbidden cry,
As I, in search of meaning's thread,
Am bound by fears and phantoms led.

In drear and dreary nights like these,
Where hope is lost in sorrow's seas,
I ponder on the nature's course,
And feel the weight of life's remorse.

What purpose lies in shadows deep?
What dreams persist in deathless sleep?
For every answer found in vain,
Leads back to night's eternal reign.

Yet in the dark, a whisper calls,
A hint of light in shadowed halls,
For purpose is a phantom's game,
A fleeting, ever-changing name.

To find it, one must look within,
Beyond the sorrow, past the sin,

And in the heart, where truth resides,
Discover where one's meaning hides.

In my embrace, this truth I glean,
That life's dark path, though seldom seen,
May lead to purpose undefined,
A journey shaped by heart and mind.

So in this search for purpose, true,
Through night's abyss and morning's dew,
I'll wander on, with heart aflame,
To find my place, my truth, my name.

58

WORTHLESSNESS

<pre>
    i
    am
            dust
            blown
    by
    a
            loveless
            wind
</pre>

59

THE BURDEN OF STIGMA

In shadows deep where judgment dwells,
Where whispers weave their silent spells,
There lies a weight, unseen, yet known,
A burden borne, yet rarely shown.

The world, in all its fleeting grace,
Can cast a harsh and cruel face,
On those who walk a different line,
Condemned by fear and bound by time.

Beneath the gaze of eyes unkind,
The soul retreats, the heart confined,
To corners dark where shadows reign,
And silence amplifies the pain.

The stigma's grip, a ghostly hand,
Clings tight, a force to understand,
Its whispers cold, a constant breeze,
That chills the heart and bends the knees.

In every glance, a hidden sneer,

In every word, a veiled jeer,
The world becomes a prison tight,
With walls of shame, devoid of light.

Oh, how the mind, in such a place,
Does seek escape, a fleeting grace,
Yet finds no door, no path, no way,
But to endure the endless day.

The burden grows with each new dawn,
As hope, like mist, is swiftly gone,
And in its place, a sorrow deep,
A sea of tears that none can weep.

Yet in the heart, a fire remains,
A spark of light amidst the chains,
For though the stigma wounds and scars,
It cannot dim the inner stars.

To rise above, to break the mold,
To challenge stories often told,
Requires a strength, a voice, a will,
To stand against the world so still.

For in the fight against the dark,
The soul must find its inner spark,
And cast aside the shame and fear,
To walk with pride, and persevere.

In my words, this tale is spun,
Of battles lost and battles won,
For in the end, the heart must rise,
To see beyond the world's disguise.

The burden of the stigma's weight,
May linger on, but cannot sate,
The soul's desire to be free,
To live in truth, in harmony.

So let the world its judgments cast,
And let the shadows fall and last,
For in the heart, where courage lies,
The strength to soar will always rise.

60

ISOLATION

<pre>
    islands
of
    selves
oceans
    between
each
    blink
</pre>

61

THE ELUSIVE PEACE

In life's tumultuous, swirling sea,
Where chaos reigns and calmness flees,
I seek a moment, pure, serene,
A glimpse of peace in life's machine.

The days are long, the nights are fraught,
With endless battles, battles fought,
Yet in the midst of dark despair,
A fleeting peace, beyond compare.

A breath of air, a whisper soft,
A gentle touch that lifts aloft,
The weary heart, the troubled mind,
A peace so rare, so hard to find.

The world, a storm of noise and haste,
Leaves little room for gentle grace,
Yet in the quiet, hidden space,
I find a tranquil, tender place.

A fleeting sigh, a moment's pause,

Where all the chaos gives its cause,
To silence pure, a calm embrace,
A fleeting peace, a tender grace.

Yet like a dream, it slips away,
As dawn must break the night's soft sway,
The peace I crave, so brief, so rare,
Is gone before I'm aware.

Oh, how I long for peace to stay,
To hold it close, to keep at bay,
The storms of life, the endless strife,
To live in peace, a tranquil life.

But peace, like shadows in the night,
Is fleeting, gone with morning light,
Yet in the heart, a hope remains,
To find that peace amidst the pains.

For in the search, the struggle long,
The soul grows strong, the heart a song,
And in the brief, elusive peace,
We find the strength to never cease.

To seek, to find, to hold, to lose,
The peace that life so rarely brews,
Is to embrace the human plight,
To find the calm amidst the fight.

So let the storms and chaos reign,
For in their wake, there lies the gain,
Of peace so brief, yet deeply sweet,
A fleeting rest, a small retreat.

In my words, this tale is spun,
Of fleeting peace and battles won,
For in the heart, where turmoil lies,
There's always hope for tranquil skies.

62

PANIC

walls

close

in

breath

a

stolen

bird

63

RISING FROM THE ASHES

In shadows cast by life's cruel flame,
Where sorrow, loss, and pain reside,
A spirit broken, yet untamed,
Begins the journey from inside.

Amidst the ruins, ashes cold,
Where dreams once bright have turned to dust,
A tale of courage, yet untold,
Unfolds in quiet, patient trust.

The heart, though scarred by endless strife,
Beats steady with a strength unknown,
For in the deepest wounds of life,
A seed of hope is always sown.

From depths of darkness, light will rise,
A phoenix from the fire's embrace,
To spread its wings beneath the skies,
And find anew its rightful place.

Each step, though faltering and slow,

Is guided by a will to mend,
To leave behind the undertow,
And seek the dawn beyond the end.

The path to healing, rough and steep,
Is paved with tears and silent cries,
Yet in each tear, a promise deep,
Of brighter days and clearer skies.

For resilience is a quiet force,
A river running strong and free,
It carves through rock, it charts its course,
A testament to what can be.

In every fall, in every pain,
There lies the seed of something more,
The chance to rise, to start again,
To find the strength within the core.

So let the flames of sorrow burn,
Let ashes fall and shadows reign,
For in their wake, the soul will learn,
To rise once more, to break the chain.

Through resilience, we find our way,
Through healing, we embrace the scars,
And in self-discovery, we lay
The path to reach beyond the stars.

In my embrace, this tale is spun,
Of rising from the ashes cold,
For in the heart, where hope's begun,
The greatest stories are retold.

With every step, a journey starts,
From ashes gray to skies of blue,
A testament to human hearts,
And all the strength that we accrue.

64

NUMBNESS

<pre>
        a
        glass
                    wall
        between
me
                    and the
world
</pre>

65

THE MALADY OF THE MIND

In realms where reason once held sway,
A specter creeps by night and day,
A malady that clouds the mind,
With thoughts of darkness, unrefined.

Depression's cloak, so heavy, cold,
Enshrouds the heart in shadows bold,
It whispers doubts, it spreads despair,
And leaves the soul in disrepair.

Self-esteem, once firm and bright,
Is dimmed beneath this endless night,
A voice within, so harsh, unkind,
That wounds the heart, the soul, the mind.

Hopelessness, a constant guest,
Lays heavy burdens on the breast,
The future, once so clear and grand,
Now slips like water through the hand.

Fatigue, a ceaseless, weary bane,
Drains life and light from every vein,
Each task, a mountain to ascend,
With strength and will that never mend.

And in this mire of grim afflict,
Where every joy and pleasure's tricked,
The body too does feel the blight,
As libido fades to endless night.

Desire, once a burning flame,
Is but a whisper of a name,
Anorgasmia, cruel thief,
Steals away the heart's relief.

No joy in flesh, no sweet release,
Just shadows in the dark increase,
A hollow ache, a silent plea,
For what was lost, what used to be.

Yet in this darkness, deep and wide,
There lies a spark that dares to bide,
For even in the direst hour,
The human spirit holds its power.

To seek the light, to find the way,
Beyond the night, to brighter day,
To heal the mind, to mend the heart,
To find again where hope can start.

Though shadows linger, doubts remain,
And whispers fill the mind with pain,

The journey out is paved with might,
With courage, strength, and inner light.

So though depression casts its pall,
And leaves the spirit weak and small,
Remember this: the heart can rise,
And find the light in darkest skies.

For Swift would tell, in prose so clear,
Of battles fought, of victories near,
That even in the deepest night,
The dawn will break, and bring the light.

66

SELF-DOUBT

mirror
shows

a

stranger
unworthy
of
love

67

THE AGONY OF ANXIOUS HEARTS

In shadowed glens where thistles grow,
An eerie specter roams the moor,
Aye, Anxiety, with fear's cruel glow,
Binds hearts and minds in endless tour.

The restless heart, it beats a tune,
O' worry, dread, and ceaseless frets,
In every day, from dawn to moon,
It whispers woes and deep regrets.

The mind, once clear as crystal stream,
Now churns with thoughts both wild and fraught,
And peace, once held in sleep's sweet dream,
Is by these fears so dearly bought.

A lover's touch, a tender kiss,
Once sparked a flame, a burning fire,
Now dulled by worry's cold abyss,
And passions wane, with no desire.

For anxious thoughts, they twist and turn,
They tie the soul in tightest knot,
And in the bed, where lovers yearn,
Such joys are faded, soon forgot.

Sexual desire, it fades away,
Beneath the weight of constant fear,
And moments meant for love's display,
Are lost to thoughts that none can hear.

The body's will, it does succumb,
To nervous waves and frantic tides,
And what was once a beat of drum,
Now falters, fails, and slowly hides.

Aye, even pleasure's purest form,
Is tainted by this anxious state,
As whispers dark, like winter's storm,
Do steal away love's sweet debate.

Yet in the depths of Scotland's night,
Where burns the heart with Celtic fire,
There lies a hope, a spark of light,
To rise above, to lift the mire.

For though Anxiety may bind,
And cast its shadow, cold and drear,
The heart, it seeks, it strives to find,
A way to conquer, persevere.

With courage drawn from ancient soil,
Where warriors fought and poets dreamed,

The spirit can, through tireless toil,
Reclaim the joy once lost, it seemed.

So let us raise a hearty cheer,
To battles fought and victories near,
For in the heart, both strong and clear,
Lies strength to quell Anxiety's tear.

In my words, this tale is told,
Of love, and fear, and anxious hold,
Yet through it all, the heart beats bold,
And finds its way to love's pure gold.

68

TRAPPED

wings
       clipped
    by
fear
      cannot
   reach
     the
      sky

69

THE FEAR IN SEXUAL PURSUIT

In twilight's veil where shadows blend,
A tale of passion, fears amend,
Where lovers seek the tender kiss,
Yet find in hearts a deep abyss.

The touch that once did spark delight,
Now quivers in the pale moonlight,
For fear entwines the lover's quest,
And haunts the mind, and breaks the rest.

In moments fraught with whispered sighs,
Where bodies meet and longing lies,
There lurks a specter, cold and stark,
A fear that leaves a lasting mark.

The yearning heart, in love's pursuit,
Is silenced by a dread, acute,
For what if passion's flame does fail,
And leaves the soul in sorrow's trail?

The eyes that once with fervor gleamed,
Now dimmed by doubts, by fears unseamed,
As every touch, each tender plea,
Is shadowed by uncertainty.

The fear of failure, deep and wide,
It steals the joy, the lover's pride,
And what was pure and fiercely bright,
Is dimmed within the silent night.

A trembling hand, a faltering voice,
In love's embrace, devoid of choice,
For courage fades as doubts arise,
And passion's fire slowly dies.

In my gaze, the world is seen,
Where love is pure, yet fears convene,
For in the depths of hearts that yearn,
There lies a fear, a cold concern.

Yet even in this shadowed plight,
Where love and fear in conflict fight,
The soul must seek to rise above,
To find the strength in purest love.

For though the fear may haunt the chase,
And linger in the lover's face,
The heart, when true, can overcome,
And find in love its truest home.

So let the fear be cast aside,
And let love's courage be our guide,

For in the end, the heart must lead,
To passion's flame, to love's pure creed.

In my words, this tale is spun,
Of love and fear, of battles won,
For in the heart where love is true,
The fear shall fade, and skies turn blue.

70

YEARNING

a
faint

light

seen

through

darkened

windows

71

FRACTURED THOUGHTS

In labyrinths of tangled mind,
Where threads of reason come undone,
The gods, it seems, have left behind,
A soul adrift, a shattered sun.

Once clear, my thoughts like rivers ran,
Now fractured streams, they twist and twine,
No longer chart a steady plan,
But wander paths serpentine.

O Muse, I call, restore the grace,
Of clarity that once was mine,
For now in shadows, I must chase,
The fragments lost in disarray.

A mind once firm, like marble strong,
Now splinters under weight of care,
Each thought, a note of broken song,
Disperses in the stagnant air.

The harmony of days gone by,

Is drowned beneath confusion's wave,
Coherent strains now falter, die,
In echoes of a mental cave.

No longer can I grasp the light,
Of positive or hopeful dream,
But stumble through an endless night,
A nightmare from which I can't scream.

O Mercury, swift guide of thought,
Restore my wits, my inner fire,
For in this chaos, all is fraught,
With fears that bind and never tire.

Each effort to maintain the course,
Is thwarted by an unseen hand,
A force that drives with cruel remorse,
My thoughts to scatter on the sand.

The sweetness of a focused mind,
Is lost amidst this inner storm,
A clarity I cannot find,
As reason's form begins to deform.

Yet in this turmoil, I must strive,
To piece together what I may,
To gather fragments, keep alive,
The hope of dawn's returning ray.

For even as my thoughts may break,
And scatter like the autumn leaves,
Within my heart, a strength awakes,
A will that clings, a soul that cleaves.

In my verse, this struggle stands,
Of fractured thoughts and minds at war,
Yet through the chaos, still demands,
A hope for light, for peace once more.

So let the gods hear my lament,
And guide me through this fractured land,
To shores where reason is not spent,
And coherent thoughts, once more, command.

72

APATHY

colors
    fade
        to
            gray
                even
                    the
                        sun
        a

                bore

73

LOST IN THE FOG

lost in the fog (of)
     my own mind
i wander through the
     gray
     (confusion wraps
       like a mist
around)

the (world) distorts
     and
  shapes shift
      as if
  reality itself is
   made of
      shadows
and
   whispers

i am an echo
   of (myself)
a fragment

        of a thought
lost in the fog (of)
        what (once was)
now is
        blurred

(clarity) is a fleeting ghost
a glimpse
        then gone
a flicker (of light)
        swallowed
by the haze

each step (i take)
        is tentative
a question (?)
        without an answer
seeking (seeking)
        but never
finding

the fog (itself)
        is
alive
        breathing (in)
            out
pulsing with (unseen) hearts
        and
            silent cries

i reach (out)
        and touch
nothing

    for there is
(nothing)
    to grasp
but the (emptiness)
    and the
      uncertainty

oh to (find)
    a path
to see (clearly)
    through
the (veil)
     to feel
the solid (ground)
    beneath

but lost (in the fog)
    i wander
hoping (for)
    a break
in the mist
    a way
out
    to find
      myself

again

74

EXHAUSTION

the
   bed
      a
      heavy
         magnet
            pulling
               me
                  down

75

A FLICKER IN THE DARK

In the vast, consuming dark,
Where shadows weave and nightmares bark,
There lies a flicker, faint and shy,
A spark that dares to light the sky.

Through the veil of blackened night,
Where despair reigns and steals the light,
A single ember, bold and bright,
Dances in defiance, taking flight.

In this abyss of endless gloom,
Where hope seems buried, a silent tomb,
The flicker whispers, soft and sweet,
A promise that the dawn shall greet.

It's in the smallest, simplest things,
The rustle of the robin's wings,
The gentle touch of morning's breeze,
The way the sunlight kisses trees.

These tiny sparks, they come and go,

In whispers soft, in moments slow,
Yet in their brief, ephemeral grace,
They cast a light upon my face.

For in this dark, where shadows play,
These flickers guide and light the way,
A beacon in the night's embrace,
A hint of hope, a touch of grace.

They speak of days that could yet be,
Of dreams that rise like tides at sea,
Of strength that blooms in fields of fear,
Of voices soft that I hold dear.

In the heart of darkest hour,
Where sorrow blooms in full dark flower,
The flicker whispers, "Hold on tight,
For even in the blackest night,

There lies a hope, a spark, a flame,
That softly whispers your true name,
And in the depths of all despair,
You'll find the strength to breathe, to care."

So in the dark, I clutch this light,
A fragile hope, a burning bright,
For even in the deepest pain,
A flicker promises the rain.

To wash away the night's cruel song,
To bring the dawn where I belong,
For in this dark, a spark can grow,
Into a fire, a hope to know.

And though the night is long and stark,
I hold onto the flicker in the dark,
For even in the shadows' reign,
A spark of hope can end the pain.

76

ANGER (TURNED INWARD)

fists
    clenched
        against
           myself
             a
             silent
               scream

77

ENDLESS LOOP

In ceaseless reel, the mind doth spin,
A web of thoughts both dark and grim,
Where joy once flourished, hope begins
To fade in shadows bleak and dim.

An endless loop, a cruel refrain,
Doth haunt the waking hours and night,
In patterns wrought of woe and pain,
The heart is chained, devoid of light.

What cursed spell, what fate unkind,
Doth trap the soul in such despair,
That every fleeting peace we find
Is swept away by tempest air?

Oh, cruel rumination's snare,
That doth entangle, bind the mind,
In cycles wrought of bleak affair,
Where solace we may never find.

The past's dark specters, they arise,

To cast their pall on present day,
Their whispers, filled with spiteful lies,
Doth lead the heart and mind astray.

Each thought returns, a ghostly shade,
To haunt the corridors of will,
Till every dream begins to fade,
And restless mind can find no still.

Yet in this storm, a spark doth glow,
A ember 'midst the endless night,
For in the heart's deep, hidden flow,
There lies a strength to fight the blight.

Oh, let the dawn break through the gloom,
And scatter shadows, chase the fear,
That minds ensnared in thought's dark room,
May find the path to skies more clear.

For though the loop may endless seem,
And rumination tight its hold,
Within the soul, there lies a dream,
Of breaking free, of growing bold.

So let the mind, in courage, rise,
To challenge every dark refrain,
To seek the truth 'neath gloomy skies,
And find the light in spite of pain.

In my voice, this tale is spun,
Of thoughts that twist in endless loop,
Yet through the night, we see the sun,
And rise above the mind's dark swoop.

For in the heart of human plight,
There lies a hope, a steadfast fire,
That through the darkest, endless night,
We find the strength to climb, aspire.

78

HOPE (A FLICKER)

a
single
    ember
        glimmering
            in
              the
                ashes

79

FOG OF CONFUSION

In hazy realms where memory fades,
The mind doth wander, lost and bare,
Through misty paths and shadowed glades,
Where clarity is all too rare.

A fog of confusion wraps the soul,
Obscuring thoughts once clear and bright,
The mind, adrift, without a goal,
Is swallowed by the creeping night.

Oh, Muse, what sorrow must I bear,
When recollections slip away,
When thoughts, like phantoms, fill the air,
And concentration goes astray?

The simplest task becomes a chore,
As focus wanes, and thoughts depart,
In this confusion, evermore,
The struggle burdens mind and heart.

Like drifting leaves on autumn's breeze,

My thoughts are scattered, lost in flight,
They flit and flutter with unease,
Then vanish into endless night.

In moments fraught with futile strain,
I seek the light of reason's flame,
Yet find my efforts are in vain,
For shadows hide its fleeting name.

Oh, how I yearn for days of old,
When mind was sharp, and clear as dawn,
When every thought was firm and bold,
Not tangled in this foggy throng.

Yet in this struggle, I must stand,
With heart unbowed, and spirit strong,
To strive, with courage, to command
The will to carry on, headlong.

For though confusion clouds the way,
And memory fades like evening's glow,
Within the heart, there still must stay
A strength to rise, a will to grow.

In my words, this plaint is laid,
Of minds ensnared in fog's embrace,
Yet through the mist, a path is made,
To seek the light, to find our place.

For in the heart, where courage lies,
There dwells a power, pure and true,
To pierce the fog, to clear the skies,
And bring the mind to light anew.

80

THE SILENT THIEF

How subtly steals the thief of mind,
On silent feet, his craft designed,
To rob the intellect's bright glow,
And leave a shadowed form below.

Once clear and sharp, the mind's bright fire,
Now dimmed by age or cruel mischance,
Is snuffed by forces that conspire,
To turn each thought to fleeting glance.

Oh cruel affliction, slow decay,
That strips the wit and keen insight,
Leaves in its wake a clouded day,
Where once was brilliance, now is night.

The daily tasks, so lightly borne,
Become a burden, hard to bear,
As thoughts once fleet are now forlorn,
And reason falters, lost in air.

In simple acts, confusion reigns,

The steps once known are lost and gone,
And what remains are fragile chains,
That bind the mind from dusk to dawn.

How shall we mourn the silent thief,
Who steals the mind yet leaves the frame,
And brings to life a ceaseless grief,
In daily trials, the heart's lame?

Yet in this sorrow, let us find
A deeper strength, a will to cope,
For though the mind be thus confined,
The heart can still embrace its hope.

Let kindness guide our faltering hands,
And patience mark our every deed,
For in the love that understands,
There lies the cure to meet the need.

In my own verse, this tale is told,
Of cognitive decline and pain,
Yet through the night, a light can hold,
And bring the mind to hope again.

For though the thief may silent creep,
And rob the mind of sharp array,
Within the soul, a light shall keep,
To guide us through the darkest day.

So let us cherish every thought,
And nurture each remaining spark,
For in the battle bravely fought,
The silent thief shall leave no mark.

81

EMOTIONAL PARALYSIS

In the deep caverns of the mind,
Where shadows dance and fears unwind,
There lies a state so cold and stark,
A soul adrift, a shipless bark.

Emotional paralysis, thy name,
A silent specter, free of blame,
Thou bind'st the heart in frozen chain,
And leav'st the spirit wracked with pain.

No forward step, no backward glance,
In stasis held, a tragic trance,
The will is caught in icy grip,
A fate decreed, a cruel slip.

Oh, how the dreams of yesteryear,
Now frozen echoes, faint and drear,
Do haunt the corridors of thought,
Where once with passion they were wrought.

What phantoms hold the spirit bound,

In webs of sorrow tightly wound?
What unseen force, what chilling hand,
Commands the heart to silent stand?

The future looms, a distant shore,
Yet oars are stilled, and sails no more
Can catch the winds of hope or change,
Adrift in seas both vast and strange.

Yet in this stillness, bleak and vast,
The heart must seek to break the cast,
For even ice must yield to fire,
And paralyzed, the soul aspire.

Oh, Muse, impart thy warming breath,
And free the heart from chilling death,
Let courage melt the frozen bind,
And clear the shadows from the mind.

In my verse, this plight is laid,
Of hearts and minds in fear arrayed,
Yet through the frost, a dawn shall break,
And bid the paralyzed awake.

For in the depths of frozen night,
There lies a spark, a hidden light,
That stirs the soul to rise anew,
And bid the heart to journey through.

So let the ice of fear dissolve,
And let the heart its strength resolve,
For in the thaw of love's embrace,
The mind shall find its rightful place.

Thus freed from chains of cold despair,
The soul shall soar, the heart repair,
And through the night, a path is shown,
To find the light, to claim the throne.

82

THE VOICE OF DOUBT

Whispers in the night,
Second-guessing shadows speak,
Heart in turmoil, slight.

83

MIND IN TURMOIL

In labyrinthine depths of night,
Where shadows weave their haunting blight,
There stirs a tempest, fierce and wild,
A mind in turmoil, fate reviled.

Conflicting thoughts, a ceaseless war,
Emotions clash on spectral shore,
In heart's abyss, where demons creep,
The soul's unrest, denied of sleep.

What dark enchantment holds me fast,
In this tumultuous, dire cast?
Where reason's light is dimly seen,
And sanity doth wear so thin?

The heart, it quakes with spectral dread,
As thoughts, like phantoms, round me tread,
In every shadow, whispers rise,
To twist the truth with cruel lies.

Oh, wretched storm within my brain,

That rends my peace and mocks my pain,
In every sigh, a bitter plea,
For solace from this agony.

Each thought, a dagger, keen and cold,
With every doubt, my fears unfold,
And passions, wild, like tempests roar,
To leave me shattered, more and more.

Yet in this chaos, dark and deep,
Wherein my troubled soul doth weep,
There lies a hope, though faint and far,
A guiding light, a distant star.

For though the mind be wracked with strife,
And shadows cut like sharpened knife,
Within the heart, a strength remains,
To bind the wounds, to heal the pains.

In my lament, this tale is spun,
Of minds in turmoil, battles won,
For in the night's relentless shade,
The soul's resilience is displayed.

So let the storm its fury cast,
For in its wake, my strength shall last,
And from the depths of dark despair,
My spirit rises, free and fair.

84

SHADOW OF THE PAST

In the quiet hours of dawn,
Where whispers of memory take flight,
I stand, a silhouette in twilight,
Haunted by shadows of the past.

These ghosts, they linger, silent yet strong,
Their touch a cold caress upon my soul,
Each breath a reminder of what once was,
And what has scarred my tender heart.

Oh, how the past weaves its intricate web,
Each thread a story, each knot a pain,
In the tapestry of my mind,
A landscape marred by trauma's reign.

I walk through days like a warrior,
Battling unseen foes in the daylight,
Yet in the stillness, they come alive,
These specters of yesteryear, these shadows.

Their whispers echo in my mind,

A chorus of doubts and fears,
A symphony of sorrow,
That plays on in the quietude of night.

But within me lies a strength,
A fire that the shadows cannot quench,
For in the heart of every storm,
There is a calm, a beacon of hope.

I gather the pieces of my broken self,
And weave them into a new song,
A melody of resilience,
A testament to the power of the human spirit.

For though the shadows of the past may loom,
And their weight may bear down on my soul,
I rise, a phoenix from the ashes,
To face the dawn, to embrace the light.

In my words, this tale is told,
Of past traumas and their lingering hold,
Yet through the darkness, I find my way,
To a brighter, more hopeful day.

For in the strength of my spirit,
And the love that surrounds me,
I find the courage to heal,
And the power to reclaim my life.

85

MENTAL EXHAUSTION

(in a world of whispers)
where thoughts
like shadows
run endless
        mazes
        of
        endless
        fears

        (oh how)
        the mind
        (sinks)
        beneath the
        weight of silent
        screams

and days stretch
    long
        long
longer still

(no rest)
for the weary
        heart
        that aches
in (infinite) circles
            of
            sleepless
            night

tiny
voices (whisper)
in corners
of the (soul)
            echo
            echo
            echoing

(please)
let
it
(end)

the body (fades)
but the mind (wants)
the peace (the rest)
        the silence
        (blessed)

oh sweet
dreams
that
slip (like sand)
through fingers

of (time)

in
this (tired)
tired
world
      let
      us (find)
      our (calm)

for in
the quiet (heart)
and
gentle (breath)
      lies the (key)
to unlock
      the cage (of)
      weariness

(oh how)
we long
for (rest)
      in
      fields
      of soft
      unending
      sleep

86

THE HEAVY HEART

Stone in my chest sinks,
Each step a weary, slow pull.
Joy, a distant dream.

87

BODY IN AGONY

The body speaks in silent screams,
A vessel of torment, raw and real,
Where every ache and throb redeems,
The ghostly whispers pain reveals.

In the marrow, sorrow burrows deep,
A crimson ache that pulses, throbs,
In joints and sinews, shadows creep,
As anguish carves its cruelest sobs.

The heart, it pounds a mournful beat,
A metronome of grief and woe,
With every pulse, the pain repeats,
A symphony of undertow.

The skin, it burns with unseen fire,
A tapestry of scars unseen,
As nerves ignite with dark desire,
In flesh, the soul's lament is keen.

Each breath, a jagged, fractured thing,

That scrapes the lungs with icy claws,
A rhythm broken, wavering,
The body's plea for respite, pause.

The bones, they grind like ancient stone,
Against the weight of weary days,
In every movement, sorrow's tone,
A testament to life's malaise.

Yet in this agony profound,
A truth emerges, stark and clear,
The body's pain, a sacred sound,
A cry for love, a call for care.

For in the depths of darkest night,
Where body, mind, and soul are torn,
There lies a glimmer, faint of light,
A whisper of a new day born.

Oh, let this suffering be heard,
In every heartbeat, every sigh,
For in the silence, truth is stirred,
And in our pain, we learn to fly.

So, bear this agony with grace,
And let the tears flow unrestrained,
For in this body's anguished space,
A strength untamed, a hope unchained.

88

ACHES WITHOUT CAUSE

In the stillness of the night,
Where shadows stretch and silence speaks,
There lies a pain, a ghostly blight,
An ache that through the body creeps.

No wound to trace, no scar to find,
Yet agony pervades the flesh,
A torment of the silent mind,
Where unseen sorrows mesh.

These aches, they dance without a name,
In joints and muscles, nerves that twist,
A phantom touch, a voiceless claim,
That in the darkness does persist.

The limbs, they tremble with the weight,
Of grief unspoken, fears untold,
As if the body bears the fate,
Of secrets that the heart does hold.

Each step, a burden, fraught with dread,

Each breath, a whisper of despair,
The body, though alive, feels dead,
A prison made of thin air.

Oh, how the heart can shape the form,
In shadows of the mind's own pain,
And in the flesh, a quiet storm,
Erupts with every thought's refrain.

For in depression's cruel embrace,
The body mirrors the soul's plight,
And aches without a cause find place,
In every moment, day or night.

Yet still, in this, a truth does lie,
That speaks of depths the mind can plumb,
Where pain and sorrow intertwine,
To leave the spirit feeling numb.

But from this place of darkened woe,
A path to healing can be wrought,
For in acknowledging the flow,
The heart and mind find what they sought.

So bear these aches with tender care,
And let the tears flow if they must,
For in the body's silent prayer,
There lies a hope, a sacred trust.

In my voice, this tale is spun,
Of pains that haunt without a trace,
Yet through the darkness, there's begun,
A journey to a brighter place.

89

STOMACH OF KNOTS

In the quiet of the morning light,
Where shadows stretch and fears ignite,
There churns within a stomach tight,
A knot of angst, a ceaseless blight.

The belly twists in silent dread,
A cauldron where anxieties spread,
Each worry, like a thread of lead,
Weaves through the gut, where hopes have fled.

No solace found in food or drink,
As every bite brings forth the brink
Of nausea's wave, where thoughts do sink,
In whirlpools dark, and hearts that shrink.

The acid burns, the cramps convulse,
A tempest in the gut's repulse,
Where every fear and grim impulse,
Converge in pain, a stark convulse.

The mind, it spirals in the night,

A dance of shadows, dark and slight,
That grips the belly, cold and tight,
In sleepless hours, devoid of light.

For in the heart of anxious days,
The body bears the mind's malaise,
And in the gut, a fire stays,
To sear the peace in myriad ways.

Oh, how to calm this raging sea,
To find a moment, still and free,
Where knots unbind and leave to be,
A tranquil space of clarity.

In my words, this plight is known,
Where stomachs twist and seeds are sown,
Of fears that in the gut are grown,
Till peace is sought, and pain is flown.

So let the breath find steady ground,
And in the heart, a calm be found,
For in this quiet, safe and sound,
The knots may loose, and souls unbound.

90

BREATHLESS

In shadows' grasp, where light does fade,
I find myself in stifling shade,
A breathless void, a silent cry,
Beneath anxiety's leaden sky.

The air, it thickens, presses tight,
Around my chest, in dead of night,
A grip unseen, yet iron-strong,
That chokes the breath, prolongs the wrong.

Each gasp a struggle, fraught with fear,
As panic's echo draws so near,
The heart, it pounds a frantic beat,
In rhythm with the fear's deceit.

The world grows narrow, vision dims,
As consciousness on edges skims,
A whirlpool of the mind's despair,
Where every breath's a gasped affair.

Oh, how the lungs do ache and strain,

In seeking peace, in fleeing pain,
Yet suffocation's cruel embrace,
Leaves naught but pallor on the face.

The mind, a tempest wild and free,
Yet trapped within, it cannot flee,
For in this prison of the soul,
Anxiety exacts its toll.

And yet, within this breathless night,
A spark of hope, a distant light,
For in the struggle, life persists,
In every breath that still resists.

Oh, my heart, once wild and free,
Now knows the chains of misery,
Yet in the darkness, seek the dawn,
Where breath returns, and fear is gone.

So breathe, though air be thin and sparse,
And face the night with courage sparse,
For in each gasp, a life renewed,
A spirit's fight, a soul pursued.

91

TENSE MUSCLES

In this mortal coil of flesh and bone,
Where shadows dance and whispers moan,
There lies a tension, dark and deep,
That seizes muscle, steals sleep.

Each fiber tight, a coiled spring,
A prisoner to the suffering,
The body's silent, ceaseless plea,
For respite from its agony.

The sinews taut, like iron chains,
Ensnaring limbs with phantom pains,
A marionette of sorrow's whim,
Where joy is fleeting, light is dim.

Oh, cruel embrace of chronic strife,
That grips and twists the thread of life,
In every motion, there's a cost,
A whispered echo of what's lost.

The shoulders bear the weight of woe,

The neck a bridge where tensions flow,
Down to the back, a rigid line,
A testament to the mind's decline.

Yet in this house of aches and fears,
Where every breath births silent tears,
There lies a strength, a fierce resolve,
To seek the balm that may absolve.

For in the pain, a truth is bared,
A soul's resilience, unprepared,
To let the darkness take its claim,
And in defiance, speak its name.

So though the muscles scream and cry,
And every movement bids to die,
There is a power, fierce and wild,
In hearts that suffer, souls exiled.

Oh, my lamenting song,
Of bodies frail and spirits strong,
In every ache, a life persists,
In every pain, a hope insists.

To find the calm within the storm,
A peace to soothe the aching form,
For in the battle, there's a grace,
A strength to face, a will to brace.

So let the muscles tense and strain,
And bear the weight of hidden pain,
For in this struggle, we are whole,
A testament to the human soul.

92

FATIGUE'S GRIP

Oh, weary soul, where light once shone bright,
Now shadows drape in endless night,
Beneath fatigue's relentless hold,
A tale of woe, in whispers told.

Each limb, a weight of leaden sorrow,
Drags through the dawn of each tomorrow,
The sun, a distant, mocking flame,
Where energy once coursed the same.

Eyes, heavy with the world's despair,
Seek solace in the vacant air,
Yet sleep, that fickle, fleeting guest,
Denies the mind its needed rest.

The heart, it beats a languid pace,
In rhythm with this slow disgrace,
Where every breath, a labor wrought,
In fields of dreams and battles fought.

Oh, my pen, wouldst thou convey,

The depth of night that shrouds the day,
The heavy cloak of fatigue's embrace,
That steals the light from every face.

For in this fog, where visions blur,
And thoughts like leaves in tempests stir,
There lies a truth, a quiet plea,
For strength to face what we must be.

To rise above this mire of woe,
And find a spark, a gentle glow,
In every step, a courage found,
In every fall, a truth unbound.

So though fatigue may grip and bind,
And steal the vigor from the mind,
There lies within a heart of gold,
A will to fight, a soul untold.

For in the darkness, light is born,
A dawn to break the endless morn,
And in fatigue's unyielding clasp,
The strength to rise, the hope to grasp.

Oh, weary soul, take heart in this,
For in the struggle, there is bliss,
A journey wrought with pain and tears,
Yet marked by love, and quelled by fears.

93

THROBBING HEAD

A tender pulse within the brow,
A beat that whispers, "Not for now,"
Yet day persists, and so does pain,
In throbbing hum, a sad refrain.

Each thought, a dagger, sharp and bright,
Each breath, a burden, day and night,
The head, a drum of endless ache,
Where silent screams the peace do break.

The world's a blur through tear-streaked eyes,
As every movement, soft, belies
The storm within, the ceaseless tide,
Where stress and sorrow do reside.

Oh, gentle soul, entrapped in woe,
Where pain's persistence will not go,
In shadows deep, where light once played,
Now only throbbing thoughts are laid.

The mind, it longs for quietude,

For moments free of solitude,
Yet in the chaos, there's a grace,
A strength within this painful space.

For though the head may throb and ache,
And every step a toil make,
There lies within a beacon bright,
A hope to guide through darkest night.

Oh, Joel, with pen so true,
To capture pain in lines anew,
In every throb, a verse unfolds,
A tale of strength, a heart that holds.

So let the ache become the muse,
In throbbing rhythm, find the clues,
To write the pain, to voice the plight,
And turn the dark into the light.

For in the throbbing, there is life,
A testament to inner strife,
Yet also to the will to bear,
To find the beauty hidden there.

In throbbing head and tender brow,
A silent strength, a solemn vow,
To face the day, to find the way,
And let the pain be but a stay.

94

THE LIGHT WITHIN

In shadows deep, where darkness dwells,
And sorrow's grip, like tolling bells,
A light persists, though faint and shy,
A spark of hope that will not die.

For every heart that's known despair,
That's felt the weight too hard to bear,
There lies within a strength untold,
A flame that burns, defying cold.

Through nights of tears and endless gloom,
Where thoughts of dread like specters loom,
Remember this: you're not alone,
In every breath, a courage grown.

The world may press with heavy hand,
And make the mind a barren land,
Yet in the soil of pain and strife,
There blooms the tender seed of life.

Oh, warrior of the silent fight,

In darkest hour, seek the light,
For every scar and every tear,
Are marks of strength, a heart sincere.

To those who've walked the path of night,
And battled shadows out of sight,
Your journey speaks of bravery,
A testament to what can be.

For in the depths of sorrow's sea,
Where hope seems lost and souls unfree,
There lies the power to arise,
To break the chains and touch the skies.

So let your spirit take its flight,
Beyond the reach of darkest night,
And know that in your heart's own song,
There beats a pulse, forever strong.

In gratitude, I pen this verse,
For every soul that's faced the curse,
Of demons dark and nights so long,
You are the light, you are the song.

Thank you for the strength you share,
For showing love in places bare,
For in your fight, we all can see,
The boundless depths of bravery.

The weight of existence may be great,
But in your hands, you shape your fate,
With every step, a victory,
Against the dark, you hold the key.

So rise, dear heart, and let it be,
Your story shines for all to see,
In you, the light of hope does dwell,
A beacon bright, a living spell.